A Practical Guide for
Integrating Civic Responsibility into the Curriculum

Second Edition

**Edited by
Karla Gottlieb and
Gail Robinson**

Community College Press ®
a division of the American Association of Community Colleges
Washington, D.C.

The American Association of Community Colleges (AACC) is the primary advocacy organization for the nation's community colleges. The association represents 1,200 two-year, associate degree–granting institutions and 11 million students. AACC promotes community colleges through six strategic action areas: national and international recognition and advocacy, learning and accountability, leadership development, economic and workforce development, connectedness across AACC membership, and international and intercultural education. Information about AACC and community colleges may be found at *www.aacc.nche.edu*.

This material is based upon work supported by the Corporation for National and Community Service under Learn and Serve America Grant Numbers 00LHEDC001 and 03LHHDC001. Opinions or points of view expressed in this document are those of the authors and do not necessarily reflect the official position of the Corporation or the Learn and Serve America program.

Cover photos courtesy Miami Dade College
and American Association of Community Colleges

Designed by VC Graphics
Printed in the United States of America
ISBN 0-87117-374-3

Contents

Preface

This curriculum guide evolved from a national service learning project of the American Association of Community Colleges (AACC) funded by the Corporation for National and Community Service (CNCS). AACC's project, *Community Colleges Broadening Horizons through Service Learning*, has worked to integrate service learning into the institutional climate of community colleges since 1994.

Recognizing that an intentional civic responsibility component was missing from many service learning initiatives, AACC selected six colleges from around the country to participate in a pilot project whose purpose was to identify service learning strategies to boost civic engagement and foster civic responsibility among community college students. The six participating colleges were Albuquerque TVI Community College, Albuquerque, New Mexico; Glendale Community College, Glendale, California; Hocking College, Nelsonville, Ohio; Mesa Community College, Mesa, Arizona; Miami Dade College, Miami, Florida; and Oakton Community College, Des Plaines, Illinois.

This guide is the result of two years of work by faculty, staff, and administrators at these colleges. The 13 contributing writers are listed on the following page. We especially want to acknowledge Gwen Nyden and Emily Morrison for their extensive contributions in writing and editing portions of this guide.

Thanks go to our colleagues who reviewed the guide in its various stages, including Lynn Barnett, Ossie Hanauer, Dave Johnson, Sharon Johnson, Nan Ottenritter, and Mary Prentice. We would also like to thank service learning practitioners from many community colleges around the country who helped "test drive" several concepts, definitions, and exercises that appear within these pages.

Finally, thank you for picking up this guide. We hope that it will give you new ideas, prompt you to revisit some long-held notions, and, in the end, benefit your students as they make their way through college, their communities, and the world.

Karla Gottlieb
Gail Robinson

Contributing Writers

Elaine Dabelko
Associate Vice President of
    Academic Affairs
Hocking College
Nelsonville, Ohio

Rudy Garcia
Director of Experiential Education
Albuquerque TVI Community College
Albuquerque, New Mexico

Virginia Gibbons
Professor of English
Oakton Community College
Des Plaines, Illinois

Karla Gottlieb
Service Learning Consultant
Miami, Florida

Jonelle Moore
English Faculty
Mesa Community College
Mesa, Arizona

Emily Morrison
Service Learning Intern
American Association of
    Community Colleges
Washington, D.C.

Gwen Nyden
Professor of Sociology
Oakton Community College
Des Plaines, Illinois

Duane Oakes
Faculty Director, Center for
    Service-Learning
Mesa Community College
Mesa, Arizona

Gail Robinson
Manager of Service Learning
American Association of
    Community Colleges
Washington, D.C.

Alan Rubin
Professor of Psychology
Oakton Community College
Des Plaines, Illinois

Margo Shea
Service Learning Coordinator
Berkshire Community College
Pittsfield, Massachusetts

Josh Young
Director, Center for Community
    Involvement
Miami Dade College
Miami, Florida

Hoover Zariani
Director, Service Learning Center
Glendale Community College
Glendale, California

Introduction

What does it mean to integrate civic responsibility into community college curricula?

For a student, it can mean:

- learning actively, not just through lecturing

- understanding the skills of active citizenship

- participating in service learning by serving in the community, and recognizing that he or she can make a difference and have an impact on one life (e.g., tutoring a child; assisting a homebound senior citizen) or many lives (e.g., implementing a neighborhood watch program; petitioning for a traffic light at a dangerous intersection)

For a faculty member, it can mean:

- giving students a chance to reflect on what it means to be a responsible member of society

- taking service learning one step further to include reflection on changed attitudes, the impact of the service experience on the individual and the community, and an increased understanding of the responsibilities of living in a democratic society

- getting personally involved in service projects, with or without students

For an institution, it can mean:

- creating a culture of service and engagement

- embracing a mission of educating students for citizenship

- taking on greater responsibility to serve the community

For a community partner, it can mean:

- creating collaborative partnerships between agencies and faculty

- informing and involving individuals in community building

- being actively involved in mentoring service learning students through reflection, guidance, and feedback

With these ideas in mind, we address the following questions in this guide: What is civic responsibility? How is it tied to service learning? How can faculty integrate concepts and exercises in a practical way that will encourage students to develop their own sense of civic responsibility? How can faculty assess the development of civic responsibility in their students?

For the purposes of this publication, civic responsibility means active participation in the public life of a community in an informed, committed, and constructive manner, with a focus on the common good. We define and discuss civic responsibility in depth in chapter 2 (service learning is defined in chapter 1).

While some people categorize civic responsibility as an ethic and civic engagement as a behavior, we use both terms in this guide, as they relate to the same general concepts of involvement in civil society. When we refer to citizens and citizenship, we do so in a broad sense, not limited to official U.S. citizenship but including all residents or members of a community.

This curriculum guide is intended to provide practical, easy-to-use applications for the widest range of faculty who would like to develop their students' citizenship skills by integrating civic responsibility concepts and practices into their college courses. We recognize that community college faculty teach courses that reflect varying levels of student development, so we have incorporated ideas that can be applied to a large number of courses, from developmental to honors. Similarly, because some faculty may have more flexibility than others in course content or structure, we present activities that can work at several levels of involvement.

We have also taken into account the various disciplines and certificate and degree programs offered at community colleges, so that faculty members from liberal arts, social sciences, physical sciences, mathematics, and vocational and technical programs all may find this guide useful and appropriate for their classes.

How to Use This Guide

As the title suggests, we have tried to create a *practical* guide. Several of us are classroom teachers and have used our own experiences with service learning in shaping this publication. As you read through the following chapters, you will move from thinking about what civic responsibility means to finding ways of integrating it into your classes and assessing the outcomes that result.

Chapter 1 looks at the need for service learning and civic responsibility in the curriculum, as a response to larger changes and trends in society and the mission of higher education. In this chapter we also ask you to consider your own classroom practices as related to civic responsibility.

Chapter 2 examines the meaning and implications of civic responsibility—how it can be defined, how teaching civic skills is highly compatible with the larger mission of higher education, and how civic responsibility is related to service.

Chapter 3 focuses on the practice of civic responsibility. Here we explore strategies that classroom teachers can use to integrate civic responsibility concepts and activities into their courses so that students come away with a greater understanding of what is expected of them as citizens in our society. These strategies, all of which can be used with service learning, range from one-time experiences or activities to multi-class or semester-long involvement.

Chapter 4 addresses assessment. Although it may prove difficult to assess the level of civic responsibility acquired by students because the goals of a civic curriculum are not as easily quantifiable as many other learning objectives, several strategies are offered that have been used successfully in community colleges.

Chapter 5 poses closing questions about the mission of your course and your college and the challenges you may face as you integrate civic responsibility into your curriculum.

It is up to you how to use this guide. Within each chapter you will find a number of exercises that are designed to get you and your students thinking about the ideas we present. We include strategies that have been tested and demonstrated to work. You may try them or adapt them in whatever ways you see fit. If you are already familiar with service learning and civic responsibility, you may decide to skim the first two chapters.

Our most important goal is to inspire you to think about different ways to get your students engaged in their communities and then to help them develop a strong sense of civic responsibility. If you find ideas and practices that do this, then we have succeeded. Good luck in your efforts to inspire your students to leave the world a better place than they found it.

"My idea of citizenship has changed as a result of service learning. Before this assignment, I believed that citizenship was only about voting and abiding by laws. We need to endorse our political efficacy…A civil society lacking active citizens possesses no enrichment, diversity, or meaning."

- Service learning student, Miami Dade College

need
for civic responsibility

Courtesy Gadsden State Community College

Chapter 1

The Need for Civic Responsibility in Service Learning

AACC defines service learning as *the combination of community service and classroom instruction, with a focus on critical, reflective thinking as well as personal and civic responsibility.*

We believe service learning offers the greatest potential for fostering civic responsibility because it provides opportunities for students to engage directly in their communities and meet community needs while enhancing their course work. It is important that, at the same time, students purposefully explore what civic responsibility means and the importance of both understanding and embracing this concept.

With the belief in the potential of service learning in mind, we decided to write this curriculum guide to address several issues and areas of concern. First, because some college students reflect the pattern of the larger society toward civic disengagement, one of the roles of higher education should be to find ways to renew and strengthen the commitment of students to civic life. It is critically important for the leadership of higher education to call on their institutions to play an active role in civic renewal. However, this renewal will not happen until faculty find ways to engage students in their communities and take the time to help them think critically about the importance of civic responsibility and their role as citizens.

Second, although there are hopeful signs that students, especially those in high school and college, are now more involved in service than in the past, it is not clear whether this service is actually cultivating a greater understanding and commitment to civic responsibility, or indeed how this could be measured (Sax 2000; Skinner and Chapman 1999). Here again, higher education can promote civic renewal through innovative initiatives such as service learning.

Third, we are concerned that not enough attention is being paid to service learning's goal of fostering civic responsibility. Although service learning continues to gain momentum as an important and far-reaching movement in higher education, it seems that faculty and service learning program coordinators are not sufficiently addressing the concept of civic responsibility with their students. Simply involving students in a service experience does not necessarily result in students gaining a better understanding of the importance and complexities of civic responsibility. It is imperative that we help faculty better understand this concept and how it relates to service learning, and provide tools to help them more purposefully integrate learning about civic responsibility into their teaching.

Finally, the increase in immigration experienced by our society in the last two decades has transformed both our communities and our college campuses. Faculty can help recent immigrants and international students find avenues toward wider participation in civil society and understand the values and beliefs that underlie our political and civic life.

Civic Disengagement in Contemporary Society

Much has been written about the growing disengagement of young people from civic life. Robert Putnam's work is often cited as evidence of the general decline in civic engagement. Based on research using a number of independent data sources, he found that older Americans—

specifically those who reached adulthood during the Depression and World War II—have been much more deeply engaged in civic life than the generations that came after them (Putnam 1996). In subsequent investigations, Putnam discovered that the trend toward civic disengagement has become even more significant since 1985 (Putnam 2000).

In 1998, the National Commission on Civic Renewal issued a report titled *A Nation of Spectators: How Civic Disengagement Weakens America and What We Can Do About It.* It concluded:

> Too many of us have become passive and disengaged. Too many of us lack confidence in our capacity to make basic moral and civic judgments, to join with our neighbors to do the work of community, to make a difference. Never have we had so many opportunities for participation, yet rarely have we felt so powerless…. In a time that cries out for civic action, we are in danger of becoming a nation of spectators.

Of special concern in much of this discussion is the disengagement of young people. Student responses to an annual nationwide survey of college freshmen conducted by the Higher Education Research Institute of the University of California–Los Angeles demonstrated the degree of disengagement from certain forms of civic life. For example, interest in politics has plummeted, as measured by students understanding the importance of being informed, voting, and discussing political affairs (Sax 2000).

According to a recent analysis of voter apathy among different cohorts of young people, there were strong indications that "political disinterest and disengagement are more widespread and deeper than was true of young people in previous decades" (Bennett 2000).

In response to these trends, the presidents of several colleges and universities from across the nation issued a declaration on the civic responsibility of higher education at a 1999 meeting of Campus Compact, a national organization of college presidents that focuses on civic engagement and service in higher education. They acknowledged that a growing number of students were participating in public and community service, but that these experiences did not necessarily lead them to embrace the duties of active citizenship. The assembled presidents identified a set of related trends among young people: a decline in voter turnout, increased feelings of indifference to political participation, a sense of cynicism, and a growing lack of trust in the political process.

In their declaration, the presidents called on their colleagues to take action against a rising tide of civic disengagement:

> Colleges and universities have long embraced a mission to educate students for citizenship. But now, with over two-thirds of recent high school graduates, and ever larger numbers of adults, enrolling in postsecondary studies, higher education has an unprecedented opportunity to influence the democratic knowledge, dispositions, and habits of

the heart that graduates carry with them into the public square.

> Higher education is uniquely positioned to help Americans understand the histories and contours of our own present challenges as a diverse democracy. It is also uniquely positioned to help both students and our communities to explore new ways of fulfilling the promise of justice and dignity for all, both in our own democracy and as part of the global community. We know that pluralism is a source of strength and vitality that will enrich our students' education and help them to learn both to respect differences and work together for the common good. (Campus Compact 1999)

Some Hopeful Signs

Despite these negative trends, there are some hopeful signs. Young people today show an increased involvement in volunteerism and community service apart from politics. There are many different routes to involvement in the community. The Corporation for National and Community Service, created in 1993, is a federal agency that supports institutional and individual efforts to provide service to local communities. Each year more than a million Americans, young and old, participate in activities and projects funded through the Corporation.

Thanks in part to the Corporation's support, there has been an increase in the number of students—at all levels of education, from primary through higher education—who perform service as part of their school experience. By 1998, a record number (74.2 percent) of college freshmen reported doing volunteer work during their senior year of high school, up from approximately 62 percent in 1988 (Sax 2000). A growing number of states and school districts require service or service learning as a condition for high school graduation.

In 1999, the Mellman Group conducted a national survey of 800 college students under the age of 31 for the Leon and Sylvia Panetta Institute for Public Policy at California State University at Monterey Bay. The survey results indicated that nearly three-quarters of college students had recently done volunteer work in an organization or for a cause they supported. This same survey also found that young people are significantly less cynical about politics and government than their elders, but they do not necessarily see these institutions as relevant to their lives or the issues that are important to them— something that service learning can help overcome (Panetta Institute 2000).

While volunteer service provides benefits to both the people who engage in it and the community agencies that receive the help, what is often missing from these experiences is structured reflection that leads to critical thinking about how the service experience is related to the life of the volunteer as an individual and as a community member.

One avenue for providing students with such structured support is service learning. While some service is performed through involvement in

extracurricular activities such as student government, clubs, religious groups, sports teams, or honor societies, a growing number of students today are introduced to service through service learning in their college classrooms. According to four national surveys conducted by AACC between 1995 and 2003, faculty at nearly 60 percent of all community colleges offer service learning. Another 30 percent of survey respondents indicated an interest in this teaching and learning strategy (Robinson and Barnett 1996; Phinney, Schoen, and Hause 2002; Prentice, Robinson, and McPhee 2003).

Service learning can be a way for students to connect or re-connect with civic society. By engaging in these activities, they may develop a set of attitudes and behaviors that is consistent with the expectations of citizenship. Sax (2000) suggests that

> It is quite possible that students are simply placing their energies where they feel they can make a difference— by getting involved in issues such as education, crime, the environment, and homelessness in their local communities. Given their frustration with political scandals and negative political campaigns, students simply may not perceive politics as an effective vehicle for positive change.

As a growing body of research indicates, service learning can be a potent civic educator (Battistoni 2000). Two different studies revealed that participating in service as an undergraduate student significantly enhanced the student's sense of civic responsibility, academic development, and overall life skill development (Astin and Sax 1998; Astin et al. 2000). A third study showed that students who performed community service were more aware of the need to become involved in the policy process, felt a greater connection to the community, and were better able to view situations from others' perspectives (Eyler, Giles, and Braxton 1997). It is important to note, however, that unless civic responsibility is *intentionally* integrated into the academic curriculum, this potential is not likely to be realized. (For examples of activities related to service learning, see box 1.1.)

Changing Demographics of Our Communities and Our Colleges

Since the early 1980s, the United States has experienced an upsurge in immigration. By the end of the 1990s, the U.S. Census Bureau estimated that there were 26.4 million foreign-born people residing in the United States, representing nearly 10 percent of the total population (Brittingham 1999).

In their community college classes, immigrants and international students may not only be learning English, but also the American way of life. When faculty offer service learning opportunities, especially those that emphasize civic engagement and foster civic responsibility, their students are given a chance to learn important lessons. As Battistoni (2000) suggests, "civic and political learning are

not innate, but the result of conscious and ongoing work by educators." While recent immigrants and international students may be accustomed to helping others in their family or ethnic community, the idea of providing service to the wider community may be an unfamiliar concept to them. (However, some countries such as Nigeria, China, Ghana, Canada, France, and Germany do have well-established national service programs similar to the

---

1.1 **Some Activities Related to Service and Service Learning**

• Take some time for self-reflection. Why did you become a teacher? Why do you teach in your discipline? Why have you integrated or are thinking about integrating service learning into your courses? Why are you interested in civic responsibility? Share your answers with your students.

• Assign Robert Coles's book *The Call of Service*, particularly chapter 2, in which he talks about different types of service. In your discussion of this reading, ask students about their own experiences with service and what led them into these activities. How does their service fit within Coles's framework? (See box 2.1 for more ideas.)

• Discuss with students what they gain by doing service as well as what their communities gain from it. Explore with them whether service is an obligation of citizenship, a privilege, a right, or none of these.

• Review the faculty case study in appendix C. Consider how faculty viewpoints on civic responsibility and involvement affect and influence students.

1.2 Some Activities Related to Our Changing Communities and Colleges

• Have your students research how your own community or college has changed since 1980. Are there more people who have emigrated from another country? What countries have they come from? What prompted their emigration? How can we use this increased diversity to strengthen our communities and our democracy?

• If you have a culturally diverse classroom, pair students together and have them talk about the concepts of citizenship and service in each of their cultures. Is there a tradition of community service? What are the criteria that establish citizenship? What is expected of citizens? If you have a diverse campus, but not a diverse classroom, work with an ESL teacher to pair students in both your classrooms. When students finish their dialogues, have them write essays or assemble the information in a publication that could be shared across the campus or the community.

• Invite speakers into your classroom who have become naturalized citizens and ask them to speak with the class about what becoming an American citizen means to them. How does living in this society differ from the country of their birth? Do they perceive the United States as a democratic society?

• In many communities there is a real need for tutors to work with people who are studying to become U.S. citizens. Find out if your local adult literacy project is looking for volunteers to work with immigrants and then recruit your students to help. For trade or technical programs, students and immigrants could work together building or refurbishing homes. Turn these into service learning projects if they relate to your course objectives.

federal AmeriCorps programs.) Service learning provides these students with a unique opportunity to become better integrated into the civic and social life of their new communities, alongside U.S.-born students. (See box 1.2 for activities related to cultural diversity.)

Just like students from other countries, U.S.-born students may not have had adequate exposure to or education about civic responsibility concepts and practices. Many of these students enter community college without a basic understanding of civic responsibility, even though some of them may have been required to do service in high school.

The increasing diversity in the classroom and the workforce provides opportunities for cross-cultural engagement and understanding. The challenge for faculty is how to make the most of this situation. By using service learning, students can explore the different meanings of civic responsibility and how to put them into practice.

This curriculum guide is a response to the challenges mentioned above. We hope that, by reading this publication, faculty and service learning coordinators will be encouraged to find new ways to promote civic responsibility on campus and in the community. Whether you are one of the thousands of higher education faculty who now use service learning or are just beginning to think about using it in your courses, we think you will find this publication helpful.

"Our students were talking about the Columbine school shooting and how they felt that the same thing could possibly happen at [their own school], which is my old high school! This shocked me and I decided that I needed to do something about violence. The [service learning] program and students motivated me to work on violence prevention in my regular paid job, which is working with at-risk youth for the city of Glendale in conjunction with the police department. I found a curriculum for a program that helps kids find alternatives to violence and, with the help of the police department, made it part of my job."

- Sociology student, Glendale Community College

defining
civic responsibility

Chapter 2

Defining Civic Responsibility

If there is a crisis in education in the United States today, it is less that test scores have declined than it is that we have failed to provide the education for citizenship that is still the most significant responsibility of the nation's schools and colleges. (Newman 1985)

If community college faculty and administrators are to address effectively the contemporary crisis cited by Frank Newman, they would do well to examine their role in instilling students with the requisite knowledge and skills to become active, effective citizens. This examination should take place on all levels, ranging from the educational institution as a whole to individual classes to specific interactions with students. We begin by considering the goals and purposes of community colleges and then explore what civic responsibility means and how it can be nurtured within the context of higher education.

Goals and Purposes of Community Colleges

In *Democracy and Education*, John Dewey ([1916] 1966) proposed two radical ideas: first, that all citizens—not just the elite—can have a life of the mind, and second, that lives that are only of the mind are not adequate to meet the demands of democracy. At a fundamental level, Dewey declared that Americans, as citizens, must be engaged both in thought and in action. He argued that education is the key to civic engagement. Therefore, institutions of learning must adequately prepare students for such activity and should be viewed as microcosms of society that should model community behavior (Ehrlich 2000, 1999).

Using service learning to develop civic responsibility allows community colleges to fulfill their basic mission of providing a quality educational experience and serving the needs of the community. Since their inception, colleges and universities in the United States have been responsible for developing both knowledge and character in their students (Colby et al. 2000; Komives and Woodard 1996). In fact, the goal of higher education is not only to prepare students for productive careers, "but also to enable them to live lives of dignity and purpose; not only to generate new knowledge, but to channel that knowledge to humane ends; not merely to study government, but to help shape a citizenry that can promote the public good" (Boyer 1987). Community colleges in particular have worked to achieve these goals while also remaining accessible and affordable to all who wish to study at these institutions.

By nurturing the development of civic responsibility in students, community colleges can help counteract citizen disengagement. To do this, however, opportunities must first exist or be created for citizen involvement in solving public problems (Boyte 1991). Many students care about the world around them but need to learn how they can affect community issues. Students also need to recognize their own voices, as well as hear and consider the voices of their fellow citizens in the decision-making process. Classroom and service activities that include discussions of civic responsibility can help students hone the skills that are vital to the success of the college and the community at large.

Community college faculty and administrators need to examine their institutional mission and assess how well they are fulfilling it. At the very core of community colleges is the call to serve all segments of society and the community (Vaughan 2000). How evident is this mission in classes, personal interactions, curriculum, and general college activities? To serve the community, institutions must help prepare students to be effective leaders and citizens who understand and embrace the concept of civic responsibility (see box 2.1).

"I definitely think our kids have learned and benefited by this program. The children learned how to apply the Cesar Chavez principles in their lives. One child told us very excitedly ... that he had almost gotten into a fight out in the school yard but that he remembered Cesar Chavez's values and decided that violence wasn't the way to resolve the issue. He said that he talked it out with the other boy and they decided on a compromise. He was very proud because he finally understood why Cesar didn't believe in violence. He said he felt much better after fixing the problem than he does after a fight."

- Social science student, Glendale Community College

2.1 Personal History of Civic Responsibility

This exercise is designed to help you understand your students' backgrounds regarding service and civic responsibility. It is a good idea to use this exercise early in the academic term, before your students have begun any service assignments.

Give students these questions or similar ones and ask them to respond in a short one- or two-page written essay. In a subsequent class session, ask students to pair up and share their personal histories with each other, or present them in class by reading their essays and showing any photos or other visual aids they may wish to share. Then lead a classroom discussion on similarities and differences among students.

1. What has been your history of service or civic involvement as a child, teenager, young adult, or adult? If you have not participated in service, describe some examples of service of which you were aware.

2. Did you participate with your family in any regular service projects? If so, what were they? What were your feelings about participating in service at that time?

3. Were you involved in service with any other organizations, such as church, synagogue, temple, mosque, youth league, Boys and Girls Clubs, Girl Scouts or Boy Scouts, or elementary school? If so, how?

4. If you were involved at an early age, do you think it affected the service you do today? Did it affect your desire to serve? Positively or negatively?

5. How has service in the community affected you, your family, or someone you know?

6. Would you classify yourself as someone who has a strong sense of civic responsibility? Why or why not?

Now consider the questions above in terms of your own personal history of civic responsibility. Whether you are a faculty member, service learning coordinator, or agency supervisor, it is important to discuss your service experiences with students and your colleagues. After answering these questions and sharing them with others, consider doing a service project of your own. Select an agency whose mission interests you and dedicate a regular number of hours there each week over a period of time. Be sure to reflect on your involvement, either in a journal or in discussions with students, colleagues, or others.

What Does Civic Responsibility Mean?

Attempting to define civic responsibility can be a daunting task because of frequently overlapping constructs, values, and interpretations. Indeed, the very mention of the term *civic responsibility* evokes notions of what it means to live in a democracy, in addition to the complementary ideas of citizenship, social responsibility, civic engagement, and community involvement.

In constructing a working definition of civic responsibility for this guide, we chose to depict it as an overarching concept that encompasses civic engagement and what it means to be a citizen:

Civic responsibility means *active participation in the public life of a community in an informed, committed, and constructive manner, with a focus on the common good.*

We encourage you to work with your students to reshape or change this definition entirely to formulate one that works for your class. For example, is anything missing from the definition? What about concepts such as social justice, social change, or respecting the rights of others? Who decides what the "common good" is? Does the notion of the common good include respecting and protecting the rights of others? Does this definition only work in a democracy? Given the working definition, how can faculty make civic responsibility an integral part of their curriculum and potentially affect student learning outcomes?

Other definitions of civic responsibility often exhibit some or all of the following characteristics:

- Addressing society's problems in an informed manner

- Showing respect as well as dissent for laws

- Recognizing the difference between legally defined and culturally defined citizenship

- Engaging in an active process that goes beyond passive citizenship

- Establishing a balance between rights and responsibilities

- Understanding the concept of the common good and who defines it

- Being able to negotiate differences

- Involving the community in decision-making processes

- Embracing the concept of participatory democracy

- Questioning governmental policies and practices

- Determining ways to alter public policy

- Exhibiting stewardship, i.e., being responsible for one's community

- Recognizing the value and human dignity of each person

- Reaching varying degrees of political awareness and advocacy, ranging from basic knowledge (e.g., knowing the local mayor's name) to developing a voice and making oneself heard

As you work with your students to define civic responsibility, you might find the activities in boxes 2.2 and 2.3 helpful. In addition to these activities, we have provided a variety of tools, exercises, and activities in chapters 3 and 4 and appendix C to help you guide active, critical reflection when using service learning as a teaching strategy.

One Student's Story

Malu Alfaro is an example of one student who took to heart service learning's call to action. A single mother of four who emigrated from the Yucatán peninsula in the 1980s, Alfaro recognized the importance of education. She waited until she had raised her children before returning to school herself. When she did return, she excelled, earning top grades and making the honor roll in her first semester at Mesa Community College in Arizona.

Alfaro then recognized a need in her community. Despite the large population of Spanish-speaking residents, there were no Spanish-language GED preparation classes in the vicinity—so she decided to do something about it. The GED test is offered in English, Spanish, and French, but without adequate English language skills and lack of information about the Spanish-language version, many local residents were hesitant to take it. As part of a service learning project for an education class, Alfaro designed, coordinated, and implemented the college's first

2.2 Some Activities Related to Civic Engagement and Civic Responsibility

These activities can be adapted for use in a classroom or a faculty workshop setting.

• Ask students to define "citizen" and "citizenship."

• Have students define civic responsibility from individual, family, community, national, and global perspectives.

• Effective citizens possess specific knowledge, skills, attitudes, and behaviors that allow them to excel. Ask students to list as many items as possible under each category that are necessary for effective citizenship.

• Have your students discuss articles, quotations, or videos that present different images of civic engagement and communicate the message of civic responsibility (see appendix A for suggestions).

• Pose the questions, "What kind of society do we want? What can each of us do to make it that way? What role does civic responsibility play in creating the society we want?" Have students pair up and share their ideas with each other, then ask them to share with the larger group.

• Ask students how civic responsibility can be related to your course, discipline, or profession. Do certain professions model a greater sense of civic responsibility and engagement than others?

• Assign students to write their "citizenship resumé," summarizing their own personal experiences in civic engagement.

Spanish-language GED preparation class. Alfaro's class attracted 30 students on the first day, with no advertising, and by the end of the semester, 50 students had successfully completed the class.

Long after her education class ended, Alfaro continues to be involved in this project. Her daughter now teaches the GED preparation class Alfaro designed, and the success stories of students who have completed it abound. For her efforts, Alfaro received a $1,000 Coca-Cola Service Scholarship and was nominated for the Howard R. Swearer Student Humanitarian Award.

2.3 General Questions about Civic Responsibility

The following questions about civic responsibility can be used to start a class discussion, as the basis for a research project, or as the foundation for an essay about personal opinions. They can be used in class, in small groups, in faculty trainings, or as a part of a post-service reflection session. They would work well with most of the activities described in chapter 3.

What does civic responsibility mean?

What does it mean to be an effective citizen?

Why is active citizenship particularly important in a democratic society?

How can community colleges help produce effective citizens?

What is the connection between your service learning project and civic responsibility?

What is the connection between service and living in a democracy?

Once immigrants feel good about the class, Alfaro hopes they will take more classes at Mesa Community College and also encourage their children to pursue college degrees. "I want to help people who are in my situation," Alfaro said. "I want to help single moms or dads in very low-income jobs, who dream of going to college, but who don't know of the opportunities…People have a chance if they have an education" (Searer 2002; "Launching Spanish GED" 2001).

"My idea of citizenship and civil society has changed as a result of my [service learning] experience. I now feel like it is my duty to give back to the community by becoming an involved citizen. Because of this wonderful experience, I now see the positive effects service learning has on society. This has helped me to really feel as though I am a part of America."

– Service learning student,
Miami Dade College

A quality service learning experience provides meaningful service that addresses community-defined needs and course-relevant learning to the students. The challenge for faculty is to integrate, at the core of the course, civic responsibility concepts and practices that contribute to a quality service learning experience. The next two chapters provide additional suggestions on how to do this.

practice

of civic responsibility

Courtesy Richland College

Chapter 3

The Practice of Civic Responsibility

This chapter provides suggestions on how to foster civic responsibility in students by integrating civic engagement components into course curricula. Faculty should consider the following:

- What are your learning objectives in introducing service learning and civic responsibility?

- How will students' service experiences relate to the course material?

- How much time do you want to dedicate to service learning?

- How can you design your course so that student service enhances classroom learning, meets community needs, and promotes civic responsibility?

First, think about what you want students to gain from a service learning activity. Every course has a number of specific learning objectives. They may be compatible with the broader goal of developing the knowledge, skills, attitudes, and behaviors necessary to become engaged citizens.

Another way of analyzing civic responsibility is to explore the intellectual, participatory, research, and persuasive skills that one needs to be a good citizen. Table 1 describes some of the components of each of these areas. See exercise 3.16 and table 2 for examples of service learning and civic responsibility activities related to a variety of courses.

As you plan your course, think about how service activities will enhance these competencies and skills as related to your discipline and learning objectives.

Table 1	Essential Civic Competencies and Skills

SKILL	SPECIFIC ACTIVITY
Intellectual Skills	Gathering, analyzing, interpreting, summarizing, evaluating, and presenting information; categorizing information; establishing correlational and cause-and-effect relationships
	Understanding issues, their history, and contemporary relevance; identifying, describing, evaluating, and defending a position; understanding fundamental laws and the role of decision making
	Identifying criteria for making judgments
	Assessing involvement; identifying implications; identifying rights and responsibilities
	Solving problems and taking action
Participatory Skills	Influencing policies; collaborating; building coalitions; negotiating, compromising, and seeking consensus
	Making decisions; gathering information; identifying needs and resources; clarifying values
	Learning cooperatively; listening to others; working with diversity in race, gender, culture, sexual orientation, religion, ethnicity, age, and ideology
Research Skills	Using libraries, books, journals, the Internet, and other resources
	Tracking issues in the media; researching issues in the community; attending, reporting, and reflecting on meetings and hearings
	Using the media to gather and analyze information; acquiring information from groups and individuals
	Learning how to access information about various issues; judging the reliability of information and their sources; learning about point of view and bias
Persuasion Skills	Participating in student government; writing letters to newspapers and members of city, county, state, and federal governments
	Identifying group and personal interests and goals; applying legal remedies to group and personal rights and interests
	Developing a rationale to support one's point of view
	Exhibiting leadership skills; developing verbal and written skills; learning how to defend an argument
	Getting others involved in civic action

Adapted from Constitutional Rights Foundation, "Fostering Civic Responsibility through Service Learning," 2000; used with permission

Once you have determined what your objectives are, the next step is to decide how much time you want to devote to a service assignment. Some faculty may see service learning as a minor part of their course and dedicate only a single class period or a single assignment to it. Others may believe it is central to their course and will want to devote the entire quarter or semester to service learning. Most faculty fall somewhere in between these two extremes.

Because there is such a range of opportunities for fostering civic responsibility, this chapter includes a section on creating an institutional culture of civic responsibility, which lists activities that involve the college and the surrounding community. You will also find suggestions for single service activities, activities that may involve more than one class period, and finally, assignments that can take the entire academic term.

"Many people are not aware of their legal rights and government assistance programs. It caused great sadness and frustration to find out how little low-income people know about their legal rights and benefits. I will definitely continue fighting for their rights."

- Communications student, Albuquerque TVI Community College

Creating a Culture of Civic Responsibility

You might want to consider organizing one or more of the following activities on your campus to reach more students—as well as faculty, administrators, staff, and the surrounding community—and to increase the effectiveness and scope of civic engagement on your campus. An underlying goal of community colleges is to serve the community, and these activities have the potential to do just that. Include pre- and post-service reflection exercises for each activity.

• Offer a "taste of service" event for your campus. Students, faculty, staff, administrators, and sometimes families spend a day serving at different agencies. Projects that provide opportunities for teamwork (e.g., environmental cleanups, tree plantings, construction, house painting, etc.) are especially good.

• Host an environmental fair. Invite elementary schools, middle schools, high schools, agencies, and college students to learn about what different environmental agencies do and how people can get involved.

• Plan issue-specific, campus-wide forums. Students, faculty, community members, and agency partners can share information about such topics as breast cancer, substance abuse, domestic violence, homeland security, gangs, teen pregnancy, family planning, AIDS awareness, women's history, civil rights, homelessness, human rights, teen suicide, and gay rights issues. The event could be followed by service at a related agency.

- Organize a Hunger Banquet on campus. The Oxfam America Hunger Banquet engages participants in a dramatization of the unequal distribution of resources and wealth in the world. It challenges students to realize how their decisions affect others. (See appendix E for contact information.)

- Coordinate blood, food, clothing, or toy drives on campus, and follow up with service at an appropriate agency.

- Plan an off-campus project that involves technical or trades disciplines (e.g., electrical, carpentry, engineering, architecture, plumbing) where students, faculty, and staff work with groups like Habitat for Humanity or Rebuilding Together with Christmas in April to build or renovate houses for low-income individuals. (See appendix E for contact information.)

- Organize a forum on civic responsibility or a town hall meeting (see exercises 3.13 and 3.14).

How to Use Class Activities and Assignments

Exercises 3.1 through 3.12 include a number of short activities and assignments that can be carried out in a single class period. Some of these are meant to be used prior to students visiting their service sites; others may be helpful for post-service reflection. Exercises 3.13 through 3.16 are meant for longer-term service learning projects.

Diversity of all sorts is prevalent within most classrooms, including differences in levels of preparedness for college course work. Recognizing this, the exercises in this chapter can be modified for use with students in courses that range from developmental to honors. Faculty in all divisions, from general education to vocational and technical programs, should be able to adapt these exercises to the particular types of courses they are teaching.

Some of these exercises share common questions or themes. Review and adapt them as needed for your own course or situation. Some of these activities may also be appropriate for use in faculty or community partner training workshops.

"Through this learning community, I was educated about the necessity to become a more engaged citizen. My special project for this class focused on researching funding for education. As I served in a local school, I saw the evidence of funding inequality and the need to represent those who cannot assist themselves in enhancing their educational opportunities, specifically disabled individuals."

- Education student, Mesa Community College

3.1 Pre-Service Assignment

Objective: To define civic responsibility, using references

Special requirements: Access to journals, articles, books, newspapers, and/or Web sites that discuss civic responsibility

Time required: A take-home assignment requiring an hour or less, plus in-class discussion requiring 45 minutes or less

Directions: Ask students to define civic responsibility using at least two sources. What knowledge, skills, attitudes, and behaviors should an effective citizen have? Ask students to explain the connections they see among service, civic responsibility, and democracy.

Sample reflection: Discuss students' responses in class. Are their definitions different? How? What are some common characteristics that the students described? Do most students see connections among service, civic responsibility, and democracy?

3.2 Defining Service

Objective: To identify what service means to each individual and understand that people define it differently

Special requirements: Copies of this exercise

Time required: 20 to 45 minutes, depending on number of students

Directions: Give students a few minutes to read and rank the items below. Select one of the items for discussion and have students line up according to how they ranked it (in order from 1 to 15). Have them talk about why they ranked the items as they did. Repeat the process with two or three other items.

People define service in many different ways. Represented below are some examples of service. Study the list carefully. Place a 1 next to the action that most closely models your personal philosophy of service. Place a 2 next to the action that is the second closest to your philosophy of service, and so on, until you have ranked every item up to 15.

_____ Helping to start an after-school program for children whose parents work during the day

_____ Joining the armed forces

_____ Providing dinner once a week at a homeless shelter

_____ Talking with a friend about a social issue of importance to you

_____ Working for a candidate in a local election

_____ Painting a community mural

_____ Chaining yourself to an old growth tree as loggers enter the forest

_____ Leaving your car at home and biking to work every day

_____ Donating money to a local charity

_____ Giving blood

_____ Tutoring a migrant worker

_____ Visiting different houses of worship (churches, synagogues, mosques, temples) every week to learn about different religions in the community

_____ Adopting a child

_____ Choosing professional work that makes a difference

_____ Voting

Sample reflection: Reflection should be used to acknowledge people's different opinions. What in their history, family background, or past experiences caused them to choose the order that they did? Did the degree of personal sacrifice involved or level of engagement lead them to rank items in the way they did? Are there any circumstances under which the students would change their rankings? How do their definitions of service relate to civic responsibility?

How many different ways can they categorize the examples of service? For example, which items relate to advocacy? Which represent direct service, charity, or personal choices?

Is there a universal definition of service? If there are so many types of service, how do groups or organizations proceed with a common language of service?

Adapted from Koth and Hamilton, *Redefining Service for Long Term Social Change*, 1993; used with permission

3.3 Self-Inventory Matrix

Objective: To help students assess their strengths and weaknesses for effective citizenship

Special requirements: Copies of the matrix

Time required: 30 minutes to one hour

Directions: Distribute the self-inventory matrix. Ask students to think about themselves and then fill in each of the four boxes with words that describe their strengths and weaknesses. Ask students to think about this activity in the context of their service site. The matrix may be used either before or after the service experience.

For example, if a student served at a nursing home and really enjoyed interacting with residents but did not think she was good at it, she would write "personal interactions" or "working with different kinds of people" in the upper left box. (This would fall in the participatory skills category in table 1.) Similarly, if a student spent four hours at the library researching homelessness as part of his group's work for a homeless shelter, and he thought he was good at it but found it tedious, then he would write "research skills" or "using books and the Internet" in the lower right box. (This would fall in the research skills category in table 1.)

	WHAT I LIKE	WHAT I DON'T LIKE
WHAT I DON'T DO WELL		
WHAT I DO WELL		

Sample reflection: When everyone is finished, share with students the essential civic competencies and skills printed in table 1 or generate your own list as a class. Once you have a list, ask them how many of their strengths match the list of competencies and skills. Finally, ask them what they could do to turn their weaknesses into strengths that would enhance their effectiveness as citizens and why they believe that type of change is important.

Adapted from Shea and Mattson, *Building Citizens,* 1998; used with permission

3.4 Class Discussion on Civic Responsibility

Objective: To introduce students to the idea of civic responsibility

Special requirements: An article, quotation, or film with a theme of civic responsibility (see appendix A for suggestions)

Time required: One hour, plus advance time for students to read article, study quotation, or view film

Directions: Assign a short article, write quotations on the board, or show a film or film clip that focuses on civic responsibility.

Sample reflection: Ask students to consider some of the following questions: What are our responsibilities as citizens of our communities, our society, or the world? If you have students in your classroom who come from other countries, ask them to share with the class what expectations surround citizenship in their native lands. They could also consider what qualities make up a good citizen; what kinds of issues are public issues; and what potential solutions exist for these concerns. How do film characters exhibit examples of active citizenship? How do the quotations or articles teach us about civic responsibility? For example, students viewing *Gandhi* or *Malcolm X* or reading Dr. Martin Luther King, Jr.'s "Letter from Birmingham Jail" could research the main character's life and message and how they relate to civic responsibility.

3.5 Picture Your Community

Objective: To understand how we define our communities and why we choose the boundaries we do

Special requirements: Paper and drawing materials

Time required: 45 minutes to one hour

Directions: How do students conceptualize their own communities? Do they consist of their friends, their college, their town, their state, their country? Or do they picture a more global community? What kind of boundaries—real or imagined—do they place around their communities? One method of helping students think about this concept is to ask them to create a picture of their community. This can initially be a quick drawing in class that takes only a few minutes. After some discussion of the drawings, students may wish to elaborate on their community representations by developing a collage, display board, photographic record, or computer-generated images.

Sample reflection: Ask students to discuss their drawings. Why did they choose the boundaries they did? How have these boundaries changed over the years? In one class, a student depicted her community by drawing a picture of her house surrounded by a fenced yard. The gate to the yard was locked. Within the yard were her child and her dog. When encouraged to conceptualize a somewhat larger community, the student said that she did not want to expand her community any further because in her small rural town, everyone outside of her fence was either "stupid or drunk." When asked how she might be able to exert a positive influence on the community outside of her fence, she was quick to say, "It's hopeless." How could you as a teacher challenge this student to become more civically engaged? How could you engage your students in a discussion to respond constructively to the issues raised by this student?

Relate this exercise to community asset mapping. What resources or services are in local neighborhoods (hospitals, schools, colleges, stores, faith-based organizations)? What resources are lacking? How does their existence affect the level of safety, affluence, or individual involvement of community members?

3.6 Rights vs. Responsibilities

Objective: To understand the relationship between rights and responsibilities in a democratic society

Special requirements: None

Time required: At least one hour of outside research and 30 minutes of in-class reflection

Directions: Ask students to read the following paragraph and research the differences between rights and responsibilities and the relationship between the two.

> Living in a democratic society we have many rights that we often take for granted. We frequently fail to understand that along with rights come many responsibilities. If we do not fulfill our responsibilities, we jeopardize our rights. For example, although most of us take for granted the right of trial by jury, the majority of us complain and look for ways of getting out of serving on a jury. We want the right but we are not willing to accept the responsibility. Good citizens understand the balance between rights and responsibilities and are willing to accept and fulfill the responsibilities inherent in a democratic society.

Sample reflection: Ask students to list as many rights as they can think of that we have in a democratic society. Ask them also to list as many responsibilities as possible. Finally, ask them to think of examples of how rights are dependent on citizens upholding their responsibilities, as well as examples of instances where we have the responsibility to give up some rights for the public good.

3.7 Dialogue vs. Debate

Objective: To understand the importance of listening and empathy as fundamental citizenship skills; to understand the difference between dialogue and debate

Special requirements: None

Time required: One hour of outside research and one hour of in-class dialogue, debate, and reflection

Directions: Select a topic that students can discuss, for example, a local or national public policy issue or a school policy. Divide students into four groups of equal size. Ask each group to research the selected topic or issue on their own. During a subsequent class period, Group 1 will debate the issue from a supportive viewpoint, and Group 2 will debate the same issue from an opposing viewpoint. Groups 3 and 4 will conduct a dialogue on the issue, discussing both "sides" equally and without antagonism.

Sample reflection: Ask students to analyze dialogue and debate from a democratic/citizenship perspective. Why is dialogue an important concept in effective citizenship? Why is dialogue more conducive to civic responsibility and citizenship skills? What is consensus? How can we move from debate to dialogue when dealing with our communities' tough issues?

3.8 Report on a Model Citizen

Objective: To develop civic competencies while learning more about citizenship

Special requirements: A list of names—contemporary and historical, from the local area and around the world—of individuals whose life work reflects qualities of good or active citizenship; this list could be discipline-specific, to tie the activity more closely to course material

Time required: One or two class sessions

Directions: Ask each student to research and write a brief report or profile about one person on your list. They should include information about what the person accomplished and how this work reflected a positive contribution to the community. Each student should be prepared to share his or her findings with the class.

Sample reflection: When everyone has reported on her or his individual citizen, ask the class to consider what qualities or characteristics these individuals shared and what makes a "model" citizen. Talk about how these qualities reflect citizenship and civic responsibility. Ask students to consider what forces were influential in the development of these qualities. What key decisions did these people make? What barriers, if any, did they overcome? What lessons did they learn? What legacy did or could they leave?

If someone has immigrated to a country illegally, can he or she be a model citizen? Can a prisoner be a model citizen? What role does legal status play in determining who is a model citizen?

3.9 Higher Education's Role in Promoting Citizenship

Objective: To explore and understand the relationship among higher education, democracy, and citizenship

Special requirements: Copies of the quotation and questions below

Time required: 30 minutes to one hour

Directions: Ask students to read Alexander Astin's (1995) quotation below, then discuss it in large or small groups.

> We [higher education] educate a large proportion of the citizens who bother to vote, not to mention most of the politicians, journalists, and news commentators. We also educate all the school administrators and teachers, who in turn educate everyone at the pre-college level. And we do much to shape the pre-college curriculum through what we require of our college applicants. In short, not only have we helped create the problems that plague American democracy, but we are also in a position to begin doing something about them. If higher education doesn't start giving citizenship and democracy much greater priority, who will?

Sample reflection: With Astin's quotation in mind, think about the following questions:

- Do you think that our educational institutions are preparing students for a life of engaged, democratic citizenship?

- How does service learning play a role in giving citizenship and democracy greater priority?

- What specifically can higher education do to give citizenship and democracy greater priority?

- Will involvement in service learning necessarily foster civic responsibility in students?

- How can we create a culture of civic engagement that results in a more humane and just society?

- How can service learning and civic responsibility relate to institutional accreditation criteria?

3.10 Panel of Local Engaged Citizens

Objective: To learn more about citizen engagement

Special requirements: A list of questions relating to issues the class has been dealing with, to be given to speakers ahead of time so that they can reflect and provide richer detail

Time required: One class session, plus additional time for preparation before the panel and in-class reflection after the event

Directions: Invite a panel of local citizens who are engaged in civic life to talk to students about their experiences. The panel could be tailored for the specific class. For example, nurses who volunteer their services to provide healthcare for the homeless could talk with nursing students; carpenters or electricians who work with Habitat for Humanity could speak with building trades students; local elected officials or activists could talk with students in a political science class; or community members who have formed a neighborhood watch organization could talk with criminal justice students. The purpose of this exercise is for students to explore the concept of civic responsibility by interacting with citizens involved in their communities.

Sample reflection: Ask the students to prepare questions about civic engagement that they can ask the panel members. Afterward, ask students what conclusions they can draw about the character of civic work; the skills necessary to be engaged; any problems or challenges to be addressed; and the nature of civic responsibility, including who defines it and how each person's definition may be unique.

3.11 Civic Engagement throughout History

Objective: To understand aspects and qualities of civic engagement and social movements over time

Special requirements: A list—contemporary and historical—of individuals and political or social movements, plus access to texts and Web sites for research purposes

Time required: One or more full class sessions for discussion and reflection, plus time outside class for research

Directions: This exercise would be especially good for a history, political science, women's studies, ethnic studies, or ethics class. Ask your students to research one of the moments in American or world history where an individual or group of citizens stood up for their rights and got involved through civil disobedience or civic engagement. Some of the people or events students might consider include the following:

- Campaigns for and/or against voting and equal rights for women (e.g., Susan B. Anthony, Alice Paul, Woodrow Wilson, Gloria Steinem, Phyllis Schlafly)

- Campaigns for and/or against civil rights for African Americans (e.g., Martin Luther King, Jr., Fannie Lou Hamer, Ida B. Wells, George Wallace, David Duke)

- Campaigns for and/or against Congressional representation and voting rights for residents of Washington, D.C.

- Advocacy groups for and/or against Native Americans, the elderly, the disabled, gay men and lesbians, farm workers, neo-Nazis, the homeless

- Issue-related initiatives such as school desegregation, abortion, gun ownership, apartheid, drug legalization, states rights, nuclear power, economic globalization

- Race-related incidents that resulted in violence, from Selma or Watts in the 1960s to Cincinnati in 2001

- Ethnic cleansing and genocidal warfare in Rwanda, Bosnia, or Sudan

- International activists such as Mahatma Gandhi in India, Rigoberta Menchú in Guatemala, Aung San Suu Kyi in Burma, Patrice Lumumba in Zaire, Nelson Mandela in South Africa, Lech Walesa in Poland

- Pro- and anti-war movements, from the Civil War to Vietnam to the Gulf War

- Corporate environmental policies (e.g., Appalachian coal mines, Love Canal), activists (e.g., Erin Brockovich, Karen Silkwood), and environmental racism

- Individual or group responses to the September 11, 2001, terrorist attacks, including recovery and relief efforts

- Individual or group responses to tsunami and hurricane relief efforts in 2004 and 2005

Sample reflection: Have students research an event, topic, or person and present their findings to the class. Some in-class discussion questions could include:

1. Was your subject a good example of civic responsibility? Why or why not?

2. What was achieved by their efforts?

3. What was compromised for their achievement? Was violence involved?

4. What else might the person or group have done to further their cause?

5. Who were the most admirable people in the movement or issue you studied?

6. What qualities or skills did they demonstrate?

7. What motivated them to get involved?

8. Did they motivate other people to join their cause? If so, how?

9. What issues, if any, are compelling enough that you would risk your life for them?

3.12 One-Time Service Learning Activity

Objective: To gain first-hand experience in civic engagement

Special requirements: A curriculum-related service opportunity that can be completed in a single visit; transportation for students, either on their own or in college vehicles; waivers for off-campus travel, if necessary

Time required: One full class session or time outside of class to serve at an agency, plus preparation time and post-service reflection

Directions: Work with the college's service learning or volunteer office, or research on your own, to locate a community agency where students can perform course-related service as a class for a single day. While many agencies are reluctant to allow single visits, there are some that are willing to have a group come only once. Connect to national initiatives like the Martin Luther King, Jr., Day of Service or Make a Difference Day. Projects may include working in a soup kitchen, planting trees, participating in neighborhood cleanups, or visiting a local nursing home or senior center. Make sure that the agency supervisor takes time to orient the students and explain the needs and challenges of the site, and that the students have the opportunity to mingle with staff and clients of the agency as they carry out their service.

Before the students begin their project, have them research the following:

1. Describe the mission of the community agency. What underlying social problem(s) does it address? Why does this problem exist?

2. How could this problem be solved or reduced? What could students personally do to help address this problem?

3. How can civic responsibility help solve this problem?

4. Why is service important and how is it related to civic responsibility?

Next, have the students serve at the selected agency.

Sample reflection: Ask students what they thought they contributed to the day's activities, what they gained from their experiences, whether their experiences were positive or negative, and how the service tied into their course work. Ask students to consider what role citizens play in helping the agency fulfill its mission, and whether they have a responsibility to help others. If there are students who do not feel a sense of responsibility to others, explore with the class why these feelings exist and how they came about.

3.13 Forum on Civic Responsibility

Objective: To examine purposefully the concept of civic responsibility

Special requirements: Meeting room; flyers publicizing event; refreshments (optional); microphone, video camera, overhead or LCD projector, VCR and monitor (optional); CD player; flip chart, markers, overhead transparencies, video (optional); tables and chairs to facilitate both large- and small-group work; envelopes with paper and pens

Time required: Three to four hours of preparation time for event organizer (i.e., service learning coordinator, honor society member, student, faculty member); at least one hour and 15 minutes for event itself

Directions: The forum can have a general civic theme for community college students or can be focused on different groups, such as a family forum on civic responsibility, a forum with a group of K–12 students, or a forum focusing on community partners. All service learning students, faculty, and friends of service learning are invited to attend the forum, which may be held on campus several times each term to give as many people as possible the chance to attend. The forum uses the following format:

Step 1. Where are we headed?

Cut headlines from local newspapers that depict the breakdown in civil society (corruption, violence, anger, discrimination) and scan them into a short PowerPoint presentation. Play a melancholic song such as Tracy Chapman's *The Rape of the World* in the background. At the end of the presentation, process the experience with questions such as:

- What did you see?
- What were your reactions?
- How did the presentation make you feel?
- What problems did it bring to mind?

Step 2. What kind of society do we want?

Encourage participants to think critically about an ideal society by posing the question, "What kind of society do we want?" Have participants work in small groups, recording ideas on flip chart paper, then ask them to report back to the large group. Solicit definitions of a just society. Show an overhead or PowerPoint slide listing the following, and discuss with all participants.

What kind of society do we want?

- Human rights are respected

- The individual's dignity and worth are acknowledged

- The rule of law is observed

- People willingly fulfill their responsibilities

- The common good is the concern of all

Do participants agree or disagree with the items on the list above? How do these items differ from the ones on their own lists?

Step 3. What does civil society mean?

Ask participants to examine the idea of civil society. Describe thoughts about whether the government and private sectors positively or negatively affect civil society. Pose the questions, "What is civil society? What are its components?" Then work in small groups, report back to the large group, and discuss or share a slide to describe the concept (including the roles of government, individual citizens, faith-based organizations, school and neighborhood associations, nonprofit organizations, volunteer groups, and the private sector).

Step 4. What are democratic values?

Engage participants in recognizing the connection between citizenship and living in a democracy. Discuss how democracy depends on citizens. Ask participants how they would define democracy, and then share a slide with different definitions of democracy. Discuss what democratic values are (e.g., concepts and ideas from the U.S. Constitution and Bill of Rights).

Step 5. What makes a citizen effective?

Help participants identify effective citizens and the skills, knowledge, attitudes, and behaviors that effective citizens exhibit. Ask participants to do the following:

- Think of someone who is an effective citizen. What characteristics make the person this way? Share thoughts in small groups.

- Ask each small group to choose one effective citizen and list the characteristics that this person has.

- Have all or some of the small groups present the effective citizen they chose and the qualities of this person that fall under the four categories of skills, knowledge, attitudes, and behaviors.

Step 6. What are citizenship skills and competencies?

Prompt participants to reflect on citizenship skills and competencies. Ask, "What are the most important skills necessary to be an effective citizen?" Have them work briefly in small groups, then report back and discuss with the large group.

Step 7. What can I do to be a better citizen?

Challenge participants to reflect on how they as individuals can be better citizens and then give them several minutes to discuss this with their group.

Step 8. Write a personal action plan

Ask each person to put in writing specific, realistic actions they are willing to take to be a better citizen by drafting a "letter to myself." Give everyone a blank envelope and paper to list things he or she is willing to do to be a better citizen. Participants then put their sheets in the envelopes and address and seal them. Collect these letters and mail them to participants several months later as a reminder of their commitment.

Sample reflection: Have participants share some of the commitments they made in their letters, their reactions to the forum, and what they learned from it. Show a motivational video about the power of service if desired.

Adapted from Miami Dade College, *Forum on Civic Responsibility*, 2002; used with permission

3.14 Town Hall Meeting

Objective: To bring representatives from various social, government, education, and community-based organizations together to discuss a community need with the general public

Special requirements: Meeting space for anticipated number of people; access to copy machine for duplication of flyers, directions, invitations, programs, handouts, etc.; postage; microphone, podium, chairs, and table(s) for panelists if necessary; signage; refreshments; college letterhead if necessary

Time required: Part of several class sessions for pre-meeting planning and post-meeting reflection; several hours of students' time outside of class; two to three hours for town hall meeting

Directions: This exercise is designed as a class project for students in various courses (such as communications, sociology, psychology, speech, and marketing) to learn their course content while addressing a community need. It presents a unique service learning experience because it requires students to work in teams to plan and implement a meeting that will require representatives from various organizations in the community and a large audience to meet and discuss a social problem or public policy.

Step 1. Identify the need

Ask yourself and your students:

- Who will identify the need—instructor, community partners, or students? Allowing students to identify the need can provide a richer learning experience.

- What community need or issue will be addressed (e.g., domestic violence, hate crimes, poverty, juvenile crime, potholes, zoning, city growth)? Determining the need is a good opportunity for students to research current social problems existing in the community.

- What type of town hall meeting will this be—interactive with panelists, a sole presenter involved in discussion with the audience, or strictly informational?

- Who will be invited—community representatives, college representatives, members of the public, others?

- When and where will the meeting take place?

Step 2. Determine which learning objectives will be addressed

Consider which objectives best match the meeting's focus.

Step 3. Design the meeting

Once a community need has been identified, students should form four groups:

- Planning and organizing (responsible for logistics, correspondence, internal information gathering, invitations, guest list, media or audio/visual equipment)

- Marketing (responsible for internal and external promotion, flyers/brochures, media coverage, public service announcements, agency invitations, directions, signage)

- Donations (responsible for identifying costs for and acquiring invitations, letterhead, brochures, printing, refreshments)

- Evaluation (responsible for participant evaluation instrument design, distribution, data collection, tabulation, dissemination)

Step 4. Hold the event

All four teams participate in putting on the town hall meeting.

Sample reflection: A successful town hall meeting inspires everyone involved into realizing that they can address community issues in an active and positive fashion. Students who participate are often left with unanswered questions that arise during the meeting. Reflection may assist them in addressing those concerns. Below is a list of questions that are beneficial to ask:

- What did you learn from the town hall meeting in relation to your course?

- What did you learn from the meeting in relation to yourself?

- Did the meeting change your perception of what it means to be an active or engaged citizen? How did it change your perception of the community need or issue?

- What did you learn as a result of planning and implementing the town hall meeting? Did it help you identify or enhance your own leadership skills?

- How do the presenters influence the larger community? How are they limited in their influence? Are they engaged citizens?

- As a result of this experience, will you become further involved in community issues that affect you, or in issues that affect others?

- What can you teach others about this experience?

3.15 Project Citizen

Objective: To develop civic competencies and skills related to public policy development

Special requirements: Overhead transparencies, poster board, markers, flip charts

Time required: Three to six class sessions or more

Directions: Begin by leading a discussion with students about what issues in the community concern them. If you are uncertain about the level of their awareness about current issues, ask them to read local newspapers and write down information on pressing local issues for a week before starting the project.

Generate a list of issues or problems and either ask students to select which issue they want to investigate in depth, or assign them to groups and then have each group decide which issue to study. After the groups have been formed and they have all selected a problem to study, they should research, analyze, and organize the following information for each problem. Research can include using print, electronic, and Internet sources and interviewing government officials, nonprofit agency employees, and citizens who are affected by the issues.

Step 1. Explain the problem

Summarize the problem, covering the following:

- How serious is the problem in your community? What do people think about this problem? Whose voices are or are not being heard?

- How widespread is the problem in your community and how does it compare to other communities in your region or in the nation as a whole?

- Whose responsibility is it to handle the problem? The government, non-profit agencies, family members, or someone else?

Step 2. Examine alternative policies to deal with the problem

Summarize two or more alternative policies to deal with the problem. For each policy discussed, consider:

- What is the policy proposed?

- What are the advantages and disadvantages of the policy?

Step 3. Propose a policy to address the problem

Select one of the alternative policies discussed in step 2, a modification of one of those policies, or one of your own choosing. The policy you propose must not violate any local, state, or federal regulations or constitutional provisions. Prepare a proposal that includes a written explanation and justification for your suggested policy, encompassing:

- The advantages and disadvantages of your policy.

- A summary of which agencies or branches of government should be responsible for carrying out your policy.

Step 4. Develop an action plan

Explain how you can develop support for implementing your proposed policy within your community. Identify:

- Influential individuals or groups in your community that might be willing to support you. Describe how you might be able to gain their support.

- Individuals or groups in your community that might oppose your proposal. Describe how you might go about gaining their support.

Also include an explanation of how you could develop support for your policy with government officials. Identify:

- Government officials or agencies that might be willing to support your policy. Describe how you might go about gaining their support.

- Government officials or agencies that might oppose your policy. Describe how you might go about trying to convince them to support you.

Step 5. Present the problem and the plan

Each group is expected to make a presentation to the class on the problem they investigated, covering the first four steps in the presentation. Groups can divide up the responsibilities for presenting among all members, or choose one or two members of the group to be the spokespersons. When making the presentation, students are expected to use visuals that can easily be seen by everyone in the class (e.g., posters, overhead transparencies, video, PowerPoint).

In addition to the presentation, each group will prepare a printed booklet to be submitted to the instructor when making the presentation. This will include, in written format, research on the problem and policy solutions, as well as a list of all information sources. The material can be presented in paragraph summaries, outline format, or bullets, but it must be well organized and follow the sequence of steps outlined previously.

Sample reflection: Because the purpose of this assignment is for students to practice civic skills while researching a contemporary issue, when they have finished, ask them what they learned about the role of citizens in addressing community problems. Through discussion and writing you can help them identify what skills they used on this assignment that could be transferred to real life if, or when, they confront a problem in their own communities.

Adapted from Center for Civic Education, *We The People...Project Citizen Teacher's Guide*, 1996; used with permission

3.16 Multiple-Class Activities or Long-Term Service Learning Projects

Objective: To develop civic competencies and skills

Special requirements: Placement sites in the community where students can perform service

Time required: Variable; most service learning projects for a standard academic quarter or semester require 15-20 hours of service, although many students opt to exceed this requirement; build in additional time for reflection

Directions: Prior to the beginning of the academic term, decide how many hours of service students should complete, what type(s) of service they will do, where the service will occur, and whether service learning is optional or required for the course. The service activities should meet a community-identified need relevant to your course content. Students may do their service in groups or individually.

While using service learning to teach core concepts, it is important to plan critical reflection assignments (academic assignments that connect the service to the learning). To take reflection one step further, include components that contribute to students' understanding of civic responsibility.

Table 2 includes a variety of ideas to help you match community needs with appropriate service learning opportunities. The service learning activities listed can be implemented in different courses or disciplines over several weeks or months, and should include reflection and civic responsibility components guided by faculty and related to course objectives. In many cases, service learning projects can be interdisciplinary, and many of the examples shown can be applied effectively to several different courses.

Be sure to consider what tools or techniques you could use to assess student learning and civic responsibility skills.

Table 2 is by no means the final word on service learning projects; it simply provides a starting point for faculty to consider how their students can meet community needs while enhancing their sense of civic responsibility. We encourage you to come up with your own combinations.

Sample reflection: There are any number of ways to reflect on the service experience and gauge the learning that has taken place. Reflection can be done in class (including discussions, presentations, or exercises) or outside class (journals, essays, art projects, group projects); see appendixes B and C for some reflection resources.

In reflecting on civic responsibility, you might ask students to identify, research, and analyze a pressing community problem or issue that is addressed by the agency where they served. They could explore what role they played in addressing that problem and what responsibility they and other members of the community have in addressing other problems. Why do particular community needs exist? What systems created the needs? Are new systems needed? What would they look like?

Table 2	Service Learning Activities		
Service Activities that Address Community Needs	**Related Courses**	**Reflection Components**	**Activities that Foster Civic Responsibility Skills**
Build Habitat for Humanity house or repair Christmas in April property	Drafting, carpentry, plumbing, electrical, architecture, heating/ ventilation, sociology, political science, psychology	Produce a video documenting the construction process while students talk with residents of the house	Research and discuss low-income housing shortage; show reflection video at city council meeting; meet with homeless shelter residents and explain Habitat for Humanity program
Provide dental health or nutrition screenings at local schools or family shelters	Dentistry, dental hygiene, nursing, nutrition, culinary arts	Keep journals to be read at town hall meetings, in other classes, at college board of trustees meeting	Share with local decision makers the need for dental and health care at a young age, and statistics of low-income children who do not receive adequate care
Create and produce informational videos for nonprofit agencies	Marketing, theater arts, languages, composition, music, photography, art, video production	Distribute *Sixteen Candles* reflection exercise and have students discuss their service experiences (appendix C)	Research the need for agency services and who their clients are; show the videos to student clubs or organizations
Teach senior citizens or low-income families computer literacy skills	Computer science, information technology, business, sociology, psychology, gerontology	Produce an online journal including samples of computer work done by seniors or families, reflecting on why clients want to be computer literate	Research the digital divide and how this gap will affect poverty rates in the future; present results to local housing officials
Assist local facility with caring for injured wild animals until they can be returned to natural habitat	Natural resources, biology, zoology, environmental science, veterinary science	Research wildlife issues for class presentations; keep reflective essays or journals; hold group discussions	Verify statistics on injured and rehabilitated wild animals and share findings in class or in campus newspaper
Become writing partners with residents at local homeless shelters or with recent immigrants	Composition, ESL, communications, foreign languages	Keep journals on the personal impact of one-on-one partnering	Produce oral histories about homelessness or immigration; share with community leaders to improve relevant city policies
Design and build community playgrounds	Carpentry, welding, child development, architecture, art, engineering	Develop photo essays documenting the design/ build process and critique design aspects	Present photo essays at school board meetings to encourage more playground development

Table 2, continued

Service Activities that Address Community Needs	Related Courses	Reflection Components	Activities that Foster Civic Responsibility Skills
Provide fire safety instruction for local elementary schools	Fire science, paramedic	Write about and discuss children's reactions to presentations	Discuss with PTA the importance of parents reinforcing fire safety rules; produce and distribute fire safety handouts to PTA
Restore damaged lands, mines, and creek banks to reduce water pollution and erosion	Environmental restoration, biology, chemistry, geology	Interview local families or doctors about the health effects of pollution	Hold a town hall meeting; invite families and local industry and civic leaders to discuss possible remedies for pollution
Form individual study and sports partnerships with juveniles in local correctional facilities	Corrections, criminal justice, juvenile justice, social sciences, education, physical education, math	Create and share photo essays of kids playing sports and doing homework	Approach school district and corrections officials to make similar programs available district-wide
Start an after-school dance program for teenagers	Dance, music, theater arts, ethnic studies	Organize and present a year-end dance recital or performance	Research and discuss the performance and musical influences of different ethnic groups
Provide first aid services for campus health centers	Nursing, paramedic, allied health, anatomy, physiology, microbiology	Share experiences with other nursing or health classes; keep reflective essays or journals; participate in class presentations or small-group discussions	Research how many college students do not receive adequate healthcare and the importance of regular health screenings; share information on campus about AIDS awareness through college newspapers, art, or speakers bureau
Repair and renovate battered women's shelter	Building trades, carpentry, heating/ventilation, plumbing, electrical, women's studies, sociology, psychology, criminal justice	Hold small-group discussions on- or off-site on why domestic violence exists in our society and how to prevent it; use reflection questions (appendix C)	Look at effectiveness of local domestic violence laws and restraining orders; distribute literature on campus or to counselors about the availability of shelters
Develop environmental programming or nature trail interpretation for schools and camps	Natural resources, biology, zoology, environmental sciences, geology	Hold group discussions or give presentations in class or to other schools/camps	Research the need for environmental education for young children
Glean crops and restaurants' excess food for local food bank or pantry	Sociology, math, business, culinary arts	Discuss immigrant or migrant worker conditions and the need for gleaning	Visit local schools and housing centers to inform migrant families of services available

assessing
civic responsibility

Courtesy Miami Dade College

Chapter 4

Assessing Civic Responsibility

This chapter presents instruments designed to elicit relevant information from your students, from understanding the difference between just performing service and really practicing civic responsibility, to assessing student outcomes in terms of civic responsibility. As you evaluate student knowledge of core competencies, you can also assess their knowledge of the meaning of civic responsibility and determine whether they understand the civic component of service learning.

Before your course starts, and before your students begin their service learning activities, consider how you will measure the change in their attitudes toward civic engagement and the development of civic responsibility. In other words, how will you establish indicators of knowledge and skills gained, and attitudes and behaviors changed?

Use these instruments in addition to your regular tools for evaluating the learning of course content. Assessing civic responsibility and the concepts related to it—compassion, the political process, the meaning of citizenship, a willingness to get involved, understanding government's role in a democracy, interpreting the individual's role in a democracy—will be important as your course enters its final weeks.

These assessment instruments are meant to complement other approaches you already use. They are not the only tools you should use in evaluating your students' learning, nor are they intended to gauge the learning of course content.

The key to a successful assessment strategy is to ask answerable questions. Following are a few questions that a faculty member or service learning coordinator could reasonably ask to evaluate what their students are learning about civic responsibility (Angelo and Cross 1993).

Questions about Students

- How many students were actively engaged in their communities prior to doing service learning?

- How many were not?

- What differences are there, if any, between the two groups?

- What do the engaged students do that other students do not?

- Is there a correlation between engaged students and those who have participated in a service learning experience?

- How are the students' current service learning experiences affecting their sense of civic responsibility?

Questions about Course Content

- How much of the course content engages students in community life?

- Which elements of the course encourage students to take responsibility for some aspect of community life, and in what ways do they do so?

Questions about Teaching

- How does your teaching affect your students' ability to become responsibly engaged in their community?

- What ethical standards guide your profession or discipline, and how are they related to civic responsibility?

- What specifically should you change in your teaching to promote civic responsibility?

- Should civic responsibility be tied to your course at all?

- How should you change those specific elements of your teaching to produce the greatest positive effects on your students' ability and disposition to engage in civically responsible behavior?

Questions about Service Learning

- To what extent does service learning increase students' awareness of their civic responsibility?

- How effective are the college's partnerships with community agencies and other service sites?

- In what ways could partnerships be changed to increase their effectiveness?

- How can faculty involvement strengthen these partnerships?

"I learned that I don't want to work in a court setting. I want to work helping the person that committed the crime—not that I was unsympathetic to the victims. I feel that society can benefit more if we can help those who commit the crimes."

- Paralegal studies student, Albuquerque TVI Community College

Following are a variety of assessment tools and exercises intended to help you answer these questions. Some of these tools share common questions or themes. Review and adapt them as needed for your own course or situation.

4.1 Syllabus Analysis

The purpose of a syllabus analysis is to provide faculty with a way to assess and revise their courses to include civic responsibility. The analysis can be done collaboratively with other faculty and program administrators or submitted for review by a third party.

1. Have you identified specific course material that relates to civic responsibility?

2. Which learning outcomes directly relate to civic responsibility? Are they explicit in the syllabus?

3. Does the syllabus include a description of service learning projects or assignments and their relation to civic responsibility?

4. What are the specific opportunities for deliberate connections among your academic content, the value of civic responsibility, and community-based service experiences?

5. How will the service experience be assessed? How will it relate to the learning of course material? Will the service experience be an explicit part of determining a student's grade?

Adapted from Gelmon et al., *Assessing Service-Learning and Civic Engagement: Principles and Techniques*, 2001; used with permission

4.2 Time Capsule

The goal of this exercise is to compare pre- and post-conceptions of a service site or of individuals at that site. Ask students to answer the following questions prior to orientation to their site(s). Collect their written responses to the questions and put them into a "time capsule" for future discussion. After the students have engaged in service for a period of time, ask them to answer the questions again, this time using the words in parentheses. After students complete the post-experience part of the exercise, open the time capsule and have students discuss and analyze any differences in their pre- and post-conceptions.

1. What are your perceptions of the service site or the individuals at the site?

2. What will be (have been) the challenges related to this service experience?

3. What will be (have been) the outcomes of this service project?

4. What will be (has been) the effect of this project on you personally?

5. Does this project have the potential to result in long-term changes? If so, what?

6. How does this service experience relate to your concept of civic responsibility?

4.3 Civic Engagement across the Curriculum

Have students read the paragraph and questions below and write a response paper. Evaluate students on the following:

- How well did they articulate their ideas?

- Did they incorporate concepts from class, readings, and/or their service experiences?

- Did they address core competencies of the course?

- Did they demonstrate that they see a connection between the service and the course material?

Higher education is currently talking about the "engaged campus," and is looking at all areas to accomplish the goal. The call to engage in service-learning for the purpose of creating a civically engaged student body and campus is one that increasingly touches all departments and disciplines at the institution. In this regard, a comparison can be made to previous efforts to do "writing across the curriculum." The movement for writing across the curriculum was based in an understanding that whatever a student's major or future aspiration, he or she needed to be proficient at written communication to be effective. This meant that every discipline or department at the university should concern itself with producing students who were "good writers." In a similar vein, the current movement toward "civic engagement" assumes that just as we want students to be good writers, we want them to be good citizens. Whatever the student's major, career, or life goals, she or he will be a member of some community, and for our democracy to be maintained and to flourish, we need people who will effectively exercise their civic rights and responsibilities. All faculty need to be enlisted in this effort to improve civic education. (Battistoni 2002)

1. Do you agree or disagree with the statement above?

2. If you agree, what steps can we take to create civic engagement across the curriculum?

3. If you disagree, how and where should civic responsibility be developed at the college?

4. Are there certain disciplines in which civic engagement should not be addressed? Why or why not?

4.4 Pre- and Post-Service Student Survey

Use this survey at the beginning and end of a course and/or service experience to gauge the effect of the service on the students and their level of civic responsibility. Some items are designed for post-service use only.

Student name: _____

Course: _____

Service site: _____

Date: _____

4-Strongly Agree   **3**-Agree   **2**-Disagree   **1**-Strongly Disagree

1. I have a good understanding of the needs and problems facing the community in which I live. **4 3 2 1**

2. If everyone works together, many of society's problems can be solved. **4 3 2 1**

3. I have a responsibility to serve my community. **4 3 2 1**

4. I probably will not volunteer or participate in the community after this course ends. **4 3 2 1**

5. The idea of combining course work with service to the community should be practiced in more courses at this college. **4 3 2 1**

6. I plan to enroll in more courses that offer service learning. **4 3 2 1**

7. The service I did through this course was not at all beneficial to the community. **4 3 2 1**

8. The service aspect of this course made me aware of some of my own biases or prejudices. **4 3 2 1**

9. The service aspect of this course showed me how I can become more involved in my community. **4 3 2 1**

10. The service aspect of this course helped me to understand better the lectures and readings required for this course. **4 3 2 1**

11. As a result of my service learning experience, I have a better understanding of my role as a citizen. **4 3 2 1**

12. As a result of my service learning experience, I would encourage other students to take courses that offer service learning. **4 3 2 1**

Comments:

4.5 Service Learning Writing Assignment

This assignment provides the instructor with information about how students synthesized their service experiences with the course content.

Write a five-page paper that summarizes your service learning experience. Organize the paper in a way that you think best expresses your thoughts and feelings about the work. You must address the following areas:

1. Describe the organization or agency at which you served, including its mission and goals, its organizational structure, and where your service effort fit.

2. Give a detailed description of the work that you did (and/or continue to do), including a description of those with whom you worked, the actual activities you did, the organization's goals for your work, its goals for you as an individual, and its goal as an agency. What did you learn about the people with whom you worked or served? Do you feel differently about them now than you did when you started the project? In what ways has your service caused you to reexamine your values, beliefs, or behaviors?

3. Explain why the work is important to you and to the organization. Why does the community need exist? How do you see your participation in service learning benefiting individuals, the neighborhood, your community, your state, or your country? How does the work contribute to a civil society or the common good? How has your service learning effort affected your own sense of civic responsibility? Has your service learning experience changed your perceptions about how you can affect the lives of others?

4. In what ways has your service learning placement made the course material relevant (or vice versa)? Be specific and provide concrete examples.

5. If you could change something about this project, what would it be? How would you do it?

6. Is there anything you wish you would have known before you started your service assignment? How would that knowledge have benefited you?

4.6 Civic Responsibility Assessment Rubric

The rubric in table 3 provides another method of assessment by documenting a student's progress from a developing level of civic participation to a proficient or exceptional level over the course of an academic quarter, semester, or year. It is meant to be used on an ongoing basis to spur continual reflection by service learning students. The rubric also provides a flexible means for faculty to assess student development and understanding related to civic responsibility, because students begin at varying skill levels on the rubric's scale and learn and improve at different rates.

Prior to beginning their service learning activities, students may find themselves at any point along the rubric's continuum. Over the course of the term, with the guidance of the instructor, they may advance to the exceptional level. The instructor may grade more highly those students who reach the exceptional level or make significant progress, as assessed through reflection logs, essays, journals, presentations, and videos.

Table 3	Civic Responsibility Assessment Rubric

Elements	Level of Quality			Assessment Options
	Developing-1	**Proficient-2**	**Exceptional-3**	**Oral, Written, Visual**
Community Involvement	Student rarely engages in community activities and shows no recognition between cultural factors and community. Does not help solve community problems peacefully.	Student sometimes engages in community activities with sustained values. Starts to encourage cultural factors. Notices relationships with community. Considers resolving community problems peacefully.	Student consistently engages in community activities with sustained values. Develops participatory skills. Encourages others to recognize cultural factors and develops functional relationship with community. Helps peers to resolve problems/ differences peacefully.	▨ Reflection Log ▨ Pre/Post Essay ▨ Dialogue Journal ▨ Oral Presentation ▨ Pre/Post Video
Interpersonal Skills	Student hardly ever acknowledges diverse community issues and seldom expresses ideas or personal attitudes toward community members. No preparation for action plan. Has problems with group members.	Student becomes more involved in political issues. Identifies diverse community members. Begins to see advantages for plan of action and starts to work with other group members.	Student thoroughly enhances political knowledge of diverse community issues. Develops communication skills and expresses ideas and values. Expands personal attitudes toward community and is respectful of its diverse members. Develops plan of action and experiences the effectiveness of thoughtful group effort.	▨ Reflection Log ▨ Oral Presentation ▨ Pre/Post Essay
Model Citizenship	Student seldom challenges political and civic issues. Makes no connection between community issues and societal needs. Has no desire to participate in political issues.	Student frequently challenges political and civic issues. Makes brief connections between community issues and societal needs. Shows some compassion for less fortunate. Might contribute to political issues.	Student consistently challenges political and civic issues. Makes connection between community issues and societal needs. Is responsive to less fortunate. Desires to engage in political issues or political actions to help community members.	▨ Reflection Log ▨ Oral Presentation ▨ Pre/Post Essay ▨ Pre/Post Video ▨ Dialogue Journal
Systems Analysis	Student rarely recognizes how organizations have a direct and indirect influence on persons they serve.	Student frequently shows awareness of direct and indirect influence on persons but does not understand how they are dehumanized.	Student always demonstrates awareness of organizations that have direct and indirect influence on how persons are served or dehumanized.	▨ Pre/Post Video ▨ Pre/Post Essay ▨ Oral Presentation

Adapted from Vaughn, "Enhancing Student Development in Service-Learning with Performance-Based Assessment Rubrics," 2002; used with permission

4.7 Community Partner Evaluation

This instrument gives community partners the opportunity to provide feedback on service learning students, their attitudes toward community needs, and their sense of citizenship.

Site Supervisor Name: _____

Organization/Agency: _____

Student Name: _____

Date: _____

4-Strongly Agree   **3**-Agree   **2**-Disagree   **1**-Strongly Disagree

1. The student had a positive impact on our organization's efforts to meet community needs.   **4 3 2 1**

2. The student's work benefited our organization's clients and/or mission.   **4 3 2 1**

3. The student was an asset to our organization.   **4 3 2 1**

4. The student was sensitive to the diversity of our clients.   **4 3 2 1**

5. The student understood our organization's mission as part of the greater community.   **4 3 2 1**

6. The student exhibited attributes of an effective citizen.   **4 3 2 1**

7. We want to continue to have the college's service learning students work with our organization.   **4 3 2 1**

Comments:

reflecting
on civic responsibility

Chapter 5

A Final Reflection

Higher education has always had a responsibility and commitment to helping students become good citizens. What better place in which to carry this out than the college classroom? Faculty cannot necessarily teach people to be good or active citizens, but they can create opportunities and exercises to provide their students with the skills to do it for themselves.

This curriculum guide provides you with the rationale and tools to restructure your classroom and your courses so that they are more explicitly focused on civic engagement. If you are convinced of the need to incorporate concepts and activities that promote civic responsibility in your course curriculum, the logical next step is to revisit the mission of the course

or courses you teach. Ask yourself the following questions:

- What is the mission of your course?

- What are the learning objectives? How do they relate to civic responsibility?

- What changes do you need to make to incorporate civic responsibility into both the mission and the learning objectives?

As you rework your course and integrate some of the concepts and exercises discussed in previous chapters, consider the following:

- What are some of the outcomes or successes you hope to see?

- What are some of the challenges you think you will face as you integrate civic responsibility into your curriculum?

- What changes will you need to make to your syllabus, your assignments, and your assessment measures in order to reflect a focus on civic responsibility?

- How will you balance intended classroom learning outcomes with anticipated service and civic responsibility outcomes?

- Will you face any opposition from the college's administration, your department chair, or division dean? If so, how will you deal with it?

Once you have tackled your own course, you might want to look at the broader institutional setting. There are a number of ways in which you can promote civic responsibility among your colleagues and your students. Begin with your own department. Are there other faculty members in your department who would be open to curricular change? Does your department have a mission statement that includes civic responsibility? If not, what will it take to make a change?

After your department or discipline, think about ways to reach faculty members in other disciplines. By promoting your students' service learning activities and your own involvement in service and civic engagement, you can provide examples of citizenship to others. If there is an existing service learning program on your campus, you can work to bring about even broader changes in the institutional climate.

Finally, take a look at the mission statement of your college to see if it mentions service or civic responsibility. If not, you might want to bring together like-minded faculty and students to talk with the college's board of trustees, provost, or president about integrating civic responsibility concepts into the college's mission statement. If service is in the mission statement, you may still want to contact these important constituencies and tell them about the activities you and your students have undertaken in the community.

Faculty are in an ideal position to help students understand that they have a responsibility to become engaged citizens. How much or how little you do to make civic responsibility a part of your curriculum and your institution is up to you. We hope that this guide has inspired you to take the first step.

"The [EnviroMentor] program has taught me to become a responsible leader and backs up what I teach in class by modeling the way. Before I began to teach I would waste water incessantly, litter without care, put others down unconsciously (and sometimes consciously), and would pay little attention to safety. These are the exact opposites of the concepts the program is attempting to instill. I did not want to become a hypocrite, so I've changed my ways...For the past three months I've acted like a responsible leader and have been a contributing factor to the well-being of future generations....This experience will always be something that I treasure and that I'll never forget."

- Education student, Miami Dade College

References

Angelo, Thomas A., and K. Patricia Cross. 1993. *Classroom Assessment Techniques: A Handbook for College Teachers.* 2d ed. San Francisco: Jossey-Bass. ERIC ED No. 422 345.

Astin, Alexander. 1995. "The Cause of Citizenship." *Chronicle of Higher Education* 42(6): 1–2.

Astin, Alexander W., and Linda J. Sax. 1998. "How Undergraduates Are Affected by Service Participation." *Journal of College Student Development* 39(3): 251–263.

Astin, Alexander W., Lori J. Vogelgesang, Elaine K. Ikeda, and Jennifer A. Yee. 2000. *How Service Learning Affects Students.* Los Angeles: UCLA Higher Education Research Institute. ERIC ED No. 445 577.

Battistoni, Richard M. 2000. "Service Learning and Civic Education." In *Education for Civic Engagement in Democracy: Service Learning and Other Promising Practices,* ed. Sheilah Mann and John J. Patrick. Bloomington, Ind.: ERIC Clearinghouse for Social Studies/Social Science Education. ERIC ED No. 447 065.

———. 2002. *Civic Engagement Across the Curriculum: A Resource Book for Service-Learning Faculty in All Disciplines.* Providence, R.I.: Campus Compact.

Bennett, Stephen Earl. 2000. "Political Apathy and Avoidance of News Media Among Generations X and Y: America's Continuing Problem." In *Education for Civic Engagement in Democracy: Service Learning and Other Promising Practices,* ed. Sheilah Mann and John J. Patrick. Bloomington, Ind.: ERIC Clearinghouse for Social Studies/Social Science Education. ERIC ED No. 447 065.

Boyer, Ernest L. 1987. *College: The Undergraduate Experience in America.* New York: Harper and Row. ERIC ED No. 279 259.

Boyte, Harry C. 1991. "Community Service and Civic Education." *Phi Delta Kappan* 73: 765–767.

Brittingham, Angela. 1999. "The Foreign-Born Population in the United States." In *Current Population Reports.* Washington, D.C.: U.S. Census Bureau.

Campus Compact. 1999. *Presidents' Fourth of July Declaration on the Civic Responsibility of Higher Education.* Internet: *http://www.compact.org/ presidential/plc/declaration.html* [Accessed 16 February 2002].

Center for Civic Education. 1996. *We The People...Project Citizen Teacher's Guide.* Calabasas, Calif.: Center for Civic Education.

Colby, Anne, Thomas Ehrlich, Elizabeth Beaumont, Jennifer Rosner, and Jason Stephens. 2000. "Higher Education and the Development of Civic Responsibility." In *Civic Responsibility and Higher Education,* ed. Thomas Ehrlich. Phoenix: Oryx Press. ERIC ED No. 439 659.

Coles, Robert. 1993. *The Call of Service: A Witness to Idealism.* Boston: Houghton Mifflin.

Constitutional Rights Foundation. 2000. "Fostering Civic Responsibility through Service Learning." *Service-Learning Network* 8(1).

Dewey, John. [1916] 1966. *Democracy and Education: An Introduction to the Philosophy of Education.* Reprint. New York: The Free Press.

Ehrlich, Thomas. 1999. "Civic Education: Lessons Learned." *PS: Political Science and Politics* 32: 245–250.

————, ed. 2000. *Civic Responsibility and Higher Education.* Phoenix: Oryx Press. ERIC ED No. 439 659.

Eyler, Janet, Dwight Giles, Jr., and John Braxton. 1997. "The Impact of Service-Learning on College Students." *Michigan Journal of Community Service Learning* 4: 5–15.

Gelmon, Sherril B., Barbara A. Holland, Amy Driscoll, Amy Spring, and Seanna Kerrigan. 2001. *Assessing Service-Learning and Civic Engagement: Principles and Techniques.* Providence, R.I.: Campus Compact.

Komives, Susan R., and Dudley Woodard, Jr., eds. 1996. *Student Services: A Handbook for the Profession.* 3d ed. San Francisco: Jossey-Bass. ERIC ED No. 423 503.

Koth, Kent, and Scott Hamilton. 1993. *Redefining Service for Long Term Social Change.* Presentation at 1993 Washington Campus Compact Conference, 26 April, Tacoma, Wash. Internet: *http://csf.colorado.edu/sl* [Accessed 16 February 2002].

"Launching Spanish GED Classes to Serve Minority Students." 2001. *The Arizona Republic,* 8 October.

Miami Dade College. 2002. Forum on Civic Responsibility. Internet: *http://www.mdcc.edu/cci/focr.html* [Accessed 17 June 2002].

National Commission on Civic Renewal. 1998. *A Nation of Spectators: How Civic Disengagement Weakens America and What We Can Do About It.* Internet: *http://www.puaf.umd.edu/ Affiliates/CivicRenewal/finalreport/table _of_contentsfinal-report.htm* [Accessed 27 October 2001].

Newman, Frank. 1985. *Higher Education and the American Resurgence.* Princeton, N.J.: Carnegie Foundation for the Advancement of Teaching.

Panetta Institute for Public Policy. 2000. *Poll Results Memorandum.* Internet: *http://www.panettainstitute.org/poll-memo.html* [Accessed 11 July 2002].

Phinney, Lisa, Mary Kay Schoen, and Ellen Hause. 2002. *Community College Engagement in Community Programs and Services.* Washington, D.C.: American Association of Community Colleges.

Prentice, Mary, Gail Robinson, and Sara McPhee. 2003. *Service Learning in Community Colleges: 2003 National Survey Results.* Washington, D.C.: American Association of Community Colleges.

Putnam, Robert D. 1996. "The Strange Disappearance of Civic America." *American Prospect* 7(24).

———. 2000. *Bowling Alone.* New York: Simon and Schuster.

Robinson, Gail, and Lynn Barnett. 1996. *Service Learning and Community Colleges: Where We Are.* Washington, D.C.: American Association of Community Colleges. ERIC ED No. 394 612.

Sax, Linda J. 2000. "Citizenship Development and the American College Student." In *Civic Responsibility and Higher Education*, ed. Thomas Ehrlich. Phoenix: Oryx Press. ERIC ED No. 439 659.

Searer, Kirsten. 2002. "MCC Offers GED Class for Spanish Speakers." *The Arizona Tribune*, 10 February.

Shea, Margo, and Kevin Mattson. 1998. *Building Citizens: A Critical Reflection and Discussion Guide for Community Service Participants.* New Brunswick, N.J.: The Walt Whitman Center for the Culture and Politics of Democracy at Rutgers University.

Skinner, Rebecca, and Chris Chapman. 1999. *Service Learning and Community Service in K–12 Public Schools.* Washington, D.C.: National Center for Education Statistics.

Vaughan, George. 2000. *The Community College Story.* 2d ed. Washington, D.C.: Community College Press, American Association of Community Colleges. ERIC ED No. 437 086.

Vaughn, Paula M. 2002. "Enhancing Student Development in Service-Learning with Performance-Based Assessment Rubrics." Ph.D. diss., Arizona State University, Tempe.

Appendix A
Films, Quotations, and Articles

Films

Following is a list of films that faculty might show their students to promote discussion and reflection about civic responsibility.

A Civil Action
American History X
Bamboozled
Crash
Dead Man Walking
Do the Right Thing
El Norte
Erin Brockovich
Gandhi
Hoop Dreams
Hotel Rwanda
It's a Wonderful Life
Malcolm X
Matewan
Mi Vida Loca
Motorcycle Diaries
Mr. Smith Goes to Washington
Norma Rae
Pay It Forward
Rashomon
Roger and Me
Schindler's List
Silkwood
Stand and Deliver
The Fisher King
The Hurricane
The Milagro Beanfield War
The Women of Brewster Place
To Kill a Mockingbird
Twelve Angry Men

Quotations

Following are some quotations related to service and civic responsibility. Using quotes can be an effective way to initiate reflective discussions or writing.

Everybody can be great because everybody can serve.
- Martin Luther King, Jr.

Service is the rent we pay for living. It is the very purpose of life and not something to do in your spare time.
- Marian Wright Edelman

I was born a citizen of a free state… however slight my voice may affect public affairs, my right to vote on them is enough to impose upon me the duty of learning about them.
- Jean Jacques Rousseau

A different world cannot be built by indifferent people.
- Horace Mann

One is not born into the world to do everything but to do something.
- Henry David Thoreau

Never doubt that a small group of thoughtful, committed citizens can change the world; indeed, it's the only thing that ever has.
- Margaret Mead

From what we get, we make a living; what we give, however, makes a life.

     - Arthur Ashe

No act of kindness, no matter how small, is ever wasted.

     - Aesop

Without community service, we would not have a strong quality of life. It's important to the person who serves as well as the recipient. It's the way in which we ourselves grow and develop.

     - Dorothy I. Height

I don't know what your destiny will be, but one thing I know: the only ones among you who will really be happy are those who will have sought and found how to serve.

     - Albert Schweitzer

I shall pass through this world but once. Any good therefore that I can do or any kindness that I can show to any human being, let me do it now. Let me not defer or neglect it, for I shall not pass this way again.

     - Mahatma Gandhi

How wonderful it is that nobody need wait a single moment before starting to improve the world.

     - Anne Frank

A thousand words will not leave so deep an impression as one deed.

     - Henrik Ibsen

Treat people as if they are what they ought to be, and help them become what they are capable of being.

     - Alice Walker

Work to make a living; serve to make a life.

     - Will Rogers

Articles

The following books are good sources for articles and readings related to civic responsibility.

Barber, Benjamin R., and Richard M. Battistoni. 1993. *Education for Democracy*. Dubuque, Iowa: Kendall/Hunt Publishing Company.

Bellah, Robert N., Richard Madsen, William M. Sullivan, Ann Swidler, and Steven M. Tipton. 1985. *Habits of the Heart: Individualism and Commitment in American Life*. Berkeley: University of California Press.

Lappé, Frances Moore, and Paul Martin Du Bois. 1994. *The Quickening of America: Rebuilding Our Nation, Remaking Our Lives*. San Francisco: Jossey-Bass. ERIC ED No. 386 812.

Shea, Margo, and Kevin Mattson. 1998. *Building Citizens: A Critical Reflection and Discussion Guide for Community Service Participants*. New Brunswick, N.J.: The Walt Whitman Center for the Culture and Politics of Democracy at Rutgers University.

Appendix B
Reflection Resources

Delve, Cecilia, Suzanne D. Mintz, and Greig M. Stewart. 1990. *Community Service as Values Education.* New Directions for Student Services, no. 50. San Francisco: Jossey-Bass.

Eyler, Janet, and Dwight E. Giles, Jr. 1999. *Where's the Learning in Service-Learning?* San Francisco: Jossey-Bass. ERIC ED No. 430 433.

Eyler, Janet, Dwight E. Giles, Jr., and Angela Schmiede. 1996. *A Practitioner's Guide to Reflection in Service-Learning: Student Voices and Reflections.* Nashville: Vanderbilt University.

Gilson, Joan, and Nan Ottenritter. 1999. *The Service Learning Journal: Writing to Learn.* Washington, D.C.: American Association of Community Colleges. ERIC ED No. 439 753.

Henry, Roger. 1995. "Sixteen Candles." In *The Tackle Box: Reflection Tools and Outcomes.* Cocoa, Fla.: Brevard Community College.

Lisman, C. David. 1999. *Integrating Reflection on Ethical Issues to Promote Civic Responsibility.* Washington, D.C.: American Association of Community Colleges. ERIC ED No. 439 753.

McKnight-Trontz, Jennifer. 2001. *The Good Citizen's Handbook: A Guide to Proper Behavior.* San Francisco: Chronicle Books.

Reed, Julie, and Christopher Koliba. 1995. *Facilitating Reflection: A Manual for Leaders and Educators.* Washington, D.C.: Georgetown University Volunteer and Public Service Center.

Shea, Margo, and Kevin Mattson. 1998. *Building Citizens: A Critical Reflection and Discussion Guide for Community Service Participants.* New Brunswick, N.J.: The Walt Whitman Center for the Culture and Politics of Democracy at Rutgers University.

Silcox, Harry C. 1993. *A How to Guide to Reflection: Adding Cognitive Learning to Community Service Programs.* Philadelphia: Brighton Press.

Zlotkowski, Edward, ed. 1997-2004. *AAHE's Series on Service-Learning in the Disciplines.* 20 vols. Washington, D.C.: American Association for Higher Education.

Appendix C
Reflection Exercises

C-1 Sixteen Candles

Use these questions as a service learning "debriefing" reflection exercise for students.

1. Describe what you learned and thought about your service project in two minutes or in two sentences.

2. Write two "feeling" words that exemplify your service learning experience.

3. Draw a picture that summarizes your experience.

4. What was the worst or most difficult thing that happened to you? Tell what you learned from the experience.

5. What was the best thing that happened? Tell what you learned from the experience.

6. Rate yourself from 1 (low) to 10 (high) for your performance. Why did you rate yourself the way you did?

7. How have you benefited from your service experience personally, academically, and occupationally?

8. What have you learned about yourself from your service learning experience?

9. What changes would you recommend in how your service site operates and how the service learning program operates?

10. Name five things that you can do to improve society.

11. How does your service experience relate to your academic work or courses?

12. Select a person you admired while doing your service learning experience. Explain what you found admirable about this person.

13. Complete this sentence: Because of my service learning experience, I am…

14. Compare or contrast your service experience with anything you have previously experienced, read about, or imagined.

15. Assume that the college is proposing to require all students to complete a 20-hour service learning experience. List the pros and cons for this proposal from both a student perspective and a community agency perspective.

16. Add your own questions.

Adapted from Henry, *The Tackle Box: Reflection Tools and Outcomes,* 1995; used with permission

C-2 General Reflection Questions

The following questions may be used for pre- or post-service reflection or on their own as part of a discussion about civic responsibility.

1. What is reflection? Why is it necessary?

2. What can we learn from service?

3. What impact can service have on your personal growth?

4. Is the government doing the same kind of work as community agencies? Should the government be expected to provide these services?

5. How does your involvement in service make you feel about yourself?

6. Why is service fulfilling?

7. What impact has the service experience had on you and on those whom you are serving?

8. Do humans have a natural inclination to help?

9. Is compassion necessary to serve?

10. Has this service experience changed your concept of civic responsibility and your desire to help others?

C-3 Charity or Social Justice: A Self-Awareness Exercise

In order for empowerment to occur, service learning programs need to move beyond a focus on charity (such as serving food in soup kitchens or visiting nursing homes during holidays). Programs that focus too heavily on charity can limit students' success at empathizing with the people they are helping. Without empathy, students might not recognize the members of the client population as valued individuals in larger society. Students may miss the opportunity to learn significantly from others in the community, individual development can be thwarted, empowerment of clients and students blocked, and ultimately societal justice not attained (Delve, Mintz, and Stewart 1990).

This reflective exercise can be used pre-, mid-, and post-service. Introduce the concepts of charity and social justice. Ask students to consider the service they do, and rank themselves on a continuum from charity to justice (either by standing in a line in the front of the classroom or by marking their place on a chalkboard). Ask the following questions:

1. Why are you at this point on the continuum?

2. What factors led you to this point?

3. Do you think you should move toward the justice end of the continuum?

4. Why or why not?

5. How do you get there?

Continue the reflection by using any of the following suggestions.

• Talk about different philosophies of service.

• Discuss the legitimacy of being at any point along the continuum; there is no right or wrong place to be. Students can move along the continuum, over time, at the pace most comfortable for them.

• Analyze the particular settings where the students serve and whether there are limits to how far along the continuum they could move.

• Discuss and get feedback from students on strategies for moving along the continuum. Do students have a responsibility to help others move from charity to social justice? How could they do this?

Adapted from Henry, *The Tackle Box: Reflection Tools and Outcomes,* 1995; used with permission

C-4 Ethics and Social Science Case Study

The following case study can be used to start discussion in a reflection session. Students can brainstorm possible conflicts that might arise during service and how to deal with them.

A service learning student working with a social caseworker learns that one of their clients is secretly playing in a band two nights a week and earning $20 per night. Since the client has a physical disability and is receiving full welfare benefits for himself and his family, he is required by law to surrender any other income to the welfare department. He is breaking the law by keeping the money. The caseworker, knowing that the welfare benefits are based on an unrealistically low cost-of-living index, does not want to report the man. The caseworker asks the student to go along with this plan. What should the student do?

Adapted from Lisman, *Integrating Reflection on Ethical Issues to Promote Civic Responsibility,* 1999; used with permission

C-5 Faculty Case Study

This case study addresses the potential conflicts faculty might face when they are civically engaged themselves or encourage their students to become more active. This can be used in a faculty training workshop to encourage reflection on their own actions and behaviors.

Faculty members from the environmental science department at a small, rural community college clashed with their institution's administration over environmental issues when the college began to undergo major construction on previously undeveloped land. The faculty believed that their integrity as educators was being undermined because their own institution was downplaying the potentially damaging environmental effects of construction. The faculty chose to go outside the institution in an effort to halt the development, contacting environmental protection agencies and raising a public relations campaign. They involved many of their students in the campaigning, both to stop the project and to rethink the long-term versus short-term needs of the college and the environment. Many of the faculty's early supporters became angry when their students got involved, believing that the faculty had coerced students into adopting their points of view.

Questions to consider:

1. Are there certain costs associated with controversial or "loaded" civic engagement at your institution?

2. How do you model democratic decision making and participation for your students when a conflict arises?

3. How can you encourage students to become civically involved without prescribing particular positions or viewpoints?

Appendix D
Bibliography

Barber, Benjamin R., and Richard M. Battistoni. 1993. *Education for Democracy*. Dubuque, Iowa: Kendall/Hunt Publishing Company.

Bellah, Robert N., Richard Madsen, William M. Sullivan, Ann Swidler, and Steven M. Tipton. 1985. *Habits of the Heart: Individualism and Commitment in American Life*. Berkeley: University of California Press.

Driscoll, Amy, Sherril Gelmon, Barbara Holland, Seanna Kerrigan, M. J. Longley, and Amy Spring. 1997. *Assessing the Impact of Service Learning: A Workbook of Strategies and Methods*. Portland, Ore.: Portland State University. ERIC ED No. 432 949.

Exley, Robert J., Karla L. Gottlieb, and Joshua B. Young. 1999. "Citizenship and Community Building." *Community College Journal* 70(3): 16–20.

Garcia, Rudy M., and Gail Robinson. 2005. *Transcending Disciplines, Reinforcing Curricula: Why Faculty Teach with Service Learning*. Washington, D.C.: American Association of Community Colleges.

Howard, Jeffrey, ed. 2001. *Service-Learning Course Design Workbook*. Ann Arbor: University of Michigan OSCL Press.

Jacoby, Barbara, and Associates. 1996. *Service-Learning in Higher Education: Concepts and Practices*. San Francisco: Jossey-Bass.

Kretzmann, John P., and John L. McKnight. 1993. *Building Communities from the Inside Out: A Path Toward Finding and Mobilizing a Community's Assets*. Chicago: ACTA Publications.

Lappé, Frances Moore, and Paul Martin Du Bois. 1994. *The Quickening of America: Rebuilding Our Nation, Remaking Our Lives*. San Francisco: Jossey-Bass. ERIC ED No. 386 812.

Parsons, Michael H., and C. David Lisman, eds. 1996. *Promoting Community Renewal Through Civic Literacy and Service Learning*. New Directions for Community Colleges, no. 93. San Francisco: Jossey-Bass.

Raybuck, Jodi, ed. 1997. *Expanding Boundaries: Building Civic Responsibility Within Higher Education*. Washington, D.C.: Corporation for National Service.

Robinson, Gail. 2000. *Creating Sustainable Service Learning Programs: Lessons Learned from the Horizons Project, 1997-2000*. Washington, D.C.: American Association of Community Colleges. ERIC ED No. 449 840.

Appendix E
Organizations and Web Sites

American Association of Community Colleges
202/728-0200
www.aacc.nche.edu/servicelearning

Campus Cares
www.campuscares.org

Campus Compact
401/867-3950
www.compact.org

Center for Civic Education
818/591-9321
www.civiced.org

Center for Information and Research on Civic Learning and Engagement
301/405-2790
www.civicyouth.org

Community-Campus Partnerships for Health
206/543-8178
www.ccph.info

Community College National Center for Community Engagement
480/461-6280
www.mc.maricopa.edu/engagement

Corporation for National and Community Service
202/606-5000
www.nationalservice.gov

Educators for Community Engagement
www.e4ce.org

Effective Practices Information Center
800/860-2684
www.nationalserviceresources.org

Habitat for Humanity
229/924-6935
www.habitat.org

National Service Inclusion Project
888/491-0326
www.serviceandinclusion.org

National Service-Learning Clearinghouse
866/245-7378
www.servicelearning.org

National Service-Learning Exchange
877/572-3924
www.nslexchange.org

Oxfam America
800/776-9326
www.oxfamamerica.org

Pew Partnership for Civic Change
434/971-2073
www.pew-partnership.org

Points of Light Foundation
202/729-8000
www.pointsoflight.org

Rebuilding Together with Christmas in April
202/483-9083
www.rebuildingtogether.org

Service Learning and Engaged Scholarship
www.evergreen.loyola.edu/~rcrews/sl

Appendix F
Supplemental Materials

F-1 Community Partner Civic Responsibility Action Plan

This action plan is intended for community partners to complete after attending a service learning or civic responsibility orientation workshop.

Please take a few moments to think about today's discussion and write notes for yourself to take back to your agency.

1. What can you do to engage students who are participating in service learning at your site?

2. How can civic responsibility be addressed in the orientation to your agency that you provide for students?

3. Does your agency address specific issues related to social justice? If so, what are they?

4. Can service learning students participate in specific opportunities where they can learn more about your organization, e.g., staff meetings, trainings, workshops, in-service opportunities, retreats, etc.? If so, what are they?

5. How can you design the on-site service learning experience so that it enhances academic course learning as well as civic engagement?

F-2 Syllabus Analysis from Different Perspectives

While syllabus creation is primarily the domain of faculty, people in other roles need to understand what goes into a syllabus and why. Select an existing course syllabus and answer the following questions from the perspectives of the different constituency groups indicated. This is a good exercise to use in a curriculum development workshop to help faculty incorporate service learning and civic responsibility concepts, expectations, and activities more clearly in their syllabi. Keep in mind that some faculty distribute course documents in addition to the syllabus that may explain service learning assignments in greater detail.

From the faculty perspective:

1. Does the syllabus describe service learning? Does it describe civic responsibility or civic engagement? If not, write appropriate language to be inserted into the syllabus.

2. Are service learning and civic responsibility clearly tied to one or more course objectives? If not, which objectives could tie to service learning and civic responsibility?

3. How will the service learning experience be assessed? Is it an explicit part of determining a student's grade? If not, how would you revise the syllabus to make it more explicit?

4. Is the syllabus clear on what the student is expected to do at the service placement site?

5. Are you sure your students will understand what is required of them in terms of service learning?

6. Are deadlines or due dates clearly identified in the syllabus (e.g., placement confirmation, service completion, reflection assignments, etc.)?

From the student perspective:

1.   Does the syllabus describe service learning? Does it describe civic responsibility or civic engagement? If not, write appropriate language to be inserted into the syllabus.

2.   Does the syllabus give you enough information about what your service learning assignment is and who to contact in case of concerns regarding your placement?

3.   Does the syllabus describe what type of reflection will occur to relate your service experience to your academic course work, social issues, and personal views? If not, write appropriate language to be inserted into the syllabus.

4.   How will your service learning experience be assessed? How will participation in service learning affect your grade?

5.   How would you describe this project to a community partner? To another student?

6.   Are deadlines or due dates clearly identified in the syllabus (e.g., placement confirmation, service completion, reflection assignments, etc.)?

From the service learning coordinator perspective:

1.   Does the syllabus describe service learning? Does it describe civic responsibility or civic engagement? If not, write appropriate language to be inserted into the syllabus.

2.   Does the syllabus include information on how to contact the service learning office? If not, where would that information fit? Write appropriate language to be inserted into the syllabus.

3.   Can you tell how the service is connected to the course work and to a student's larger role as a participant in society?

4.   Does the syllabus provide information regarding how to participate in service learning and how to choose agency sites? If not, where will students get this information?

5.   Is there enough information on the syllabus to help the student explain the project to a community partner by telephone?

6.   Are deadlines or due dates clearly identified in the syllabus (e.g., placement confirmation, service completion, reflection assignments, etc.)?

From the community partner perspective:

1. Does the syllabus describe the type of work the student must accomplish at your site?

2. What information should the instructor include in the syllabus to help prepare students to be effective at your organization?

3. What activities would you have students do at your site? Remember that the activities need to be tied to this specific course.

4. How would you explain your organization's mission to students in this course, so that they understand your role in meeting community needs?

5. In your best judgment, how would you grade students at your site for their service learning performance? Does the syllabus include procedures for you to give the instructor feedback about the students?

6. Are deadlines or due dates clearly identified in the syllabus (e.g., placement confirmation, service completion, reflection assignments, etc.)?

From the dean or department chair perspective:

1. Are service learning and civic responsibility clearly tied to one or more course objectives? If not, which objectives could tie to service learning and civic responsibility?

2. Is the service learning project connected to the overall goals of the department/division or the college's mission?

3. Are there other service learning projects that might fit into the course?

4. Is the assessment component of this syllabus (related to service learning and civic responsibility) strong enough to be defended against your college's curriculum committee?

5. Do you feel that sufficient efforts have been undertaken to reduce any liability to the college and students in this course?

6. Are deadlines or due dates clearly identified in the syllabus (e.g., placement confirmation, service completion, reflection assignments, etc.)?

F-3 Student Civic Engagement Survey

AACC developed this pre- and post-service instrument to gauge students' knowledge of and commitment to civic engagement, particularly after completing service learning as part of their course work. Some items are designed for post-service use only.

The information you provide in this survey will be used to assess your level of community involvement and civic engagement compared to other students at this college. Civic engagement means active participation in the public life of a community in an informed, committed, and constructive manner, with a focus on the common good. All of your responses and any personal information will remain confidential.

Student name or ID number: _____

Course: _____

Instructor: _____

Date: _____

1. Which of the following best describes your volunteer activity in the last 12 months?
    a. I volunteered on a regular basis
    b. I volunteered once in a while
    c. I did not volunteer

2. Which of the following have you volunteered to do within the last 12 months? (Circle all that apply.)
    a. Activities involving youth, children, or education
    b. Activities involving the elderly
    c. Activities involving public safety
    d. Activities providing health services
    e. Activities providing social services
    f. Activities for a faith-based organization
    g. Activities for an environmental organization
    h. Activities for an employee association or union
    i. Activities for a political candidate, group, or organization
    j. Other (please specify) _____
    k. None

3. Are you registered to vote in the U.S.?
    a. Yes
    b. No
    c. I don't remember
    d. I'm not eligible to vote

4. How often do you vote in local elections?
    a. Always
    b. Sometimes
    c. Rarely
    d. Never
    e. I'm not eligible to vote

5. How often do you vote in national elections?
    a. Always
    b. Sometimes
    c. Rarely
    d. Never
    e. I'm not eligible to vote

6. Have you ever written a letter to a newspaper or government official to express your opinion about an issue?
    a. Yes, within the last 12 months
    b. Yes, but not within the last 12 months
    c. No
    d. I don't remember

7. Have you ever signed a written petition related to a political or social issue that was important to you?
    a. Yes, within the last 12 months
    b. Yes, but not within the last 12 months
    c. No
    d. I don't remember
    e. I've never been asked to sign

8. Have you ever signed an e-mail petition related to a political or social issue, such as an e-mail message to which you add your name and forward to others you know?
    a. Yes, within the last 12 months
    b. Yes, but not within the last 12 months
    c. No
    d. I don't remember
    e. I've never been asked to sign
    f. I never respond to any e-mail petitions

9. Do you know the name of your community's chief elected official (e.g., mayor, tribal leader, city manager)?
    a. Yes
    b. No

10. Do you know when your town, city, or tribal council meetings are held?
    a. Yes   b. No

11. Have you ever attended a meeting of your town, city, or tribal council, or a neighborhood organization?
    a. Yes, within the last 12 months   c. No
    b. Yes, but not within the last 12 months   d. I don't remember

12. Do you know the name(s) of your state and/or national legislators?
    a. Yes   b. No

13. Have you ever worked with an individual or organization to address a problem in the community where you live?
    a. Yes, within the last 12 months   c. No
    b. Yes, but not within the last 12 months   d. I don't remember

14. If you found out that there was a problem in your community but there was no group or service agency to help, would you be the one to organize a group to address the problem?
    a. Yes   c. No
    b. Maybe

15. If an issue that you cared about surfaced in your community, would you contact any local, state, or national officials to address the issue?
    a. Yes   c. No
    b. Maybe

16. If an issue that you cared about surfaced in your community, would you consider running for public office to address the issue?
    a. Yes   c. No
    b. Maybe

17. If a candidate you believed in ran for office, would you volunteer to help in his or her campaign?
    a. Yes   c. No
    b. Maybe

18. If you had an opportunity to participate with a group of people and some of those people were of a different race, gender, ethnicity, sexual orientation, or religion than you are, would these differences make you less likely to participate in that group?

    a. Yes   c. No

    b. Maybe

19. If you found out that some students at your college were homeless, would you try to find a way to help?

    a. Yes   c. No

    b. Maybe

20. If you found out that some students at your college were homeless, would you know which community service agencies could help?

    a. Yes   b. No

21. Will you volunteer in your community in the next 12 months?

    a. Yes, definitely   c. Probably not

    b. Probably   d. Definitely not

22. At this college, how many courses have you taken that included service learning? Service learning combines community service and classroom instruction, with a focus on critical, reflective thinking as well as personal and civic responsibility.

    a. 0   d. 3

    b. 1   e. 4

    c. 2   f. 5 or more

23. If you have taken a course that included service learning, did service learning increase your knowledge of community needs and how people can address them?

    a. Yes   b. No

24. If you have taken a course that included service learning, did service learning increase your commitment to continue serving in your community?

    a. Yes   b. No

Post-service items only:

If you participated in service learning in this course this term, please answer all of the remaining questions.

25.   Did the service aspect of this course make you aware of some of your own biases or prejudices?
   a. Yes, to a great extent   c. Yes, to a minimal extent
   b. Yes, to a moderate extent   d. No

26.   Did the service aspect of this course show you how you can become more involved in your community?
   a. Yes, to a great extent   c. Yes, to a minimal extent
   b. Yes, to a moderate extent   d. No

27.   Did the service aspect of this course help you to have a better understanding of your role as a community member?
   a. Yes, to a great extent   c. Yes, to a minimal extent
   b. Yes, to a moderate extent   d. No

28.   Did the service aspect of this course help you to see how the subject matter you learned can be used in everyday life?
   a. Yes, to a great extent   c. Yes, to a minimal extent
   b. Yes, to a moderate extent   d. No

29.   As a result of your service learning experience, would you encourage other students to take courses that offer service learning?
   a. Yes   b. No

30.   Do you believe that the idea of combining course work with service to the community should be practiced in more courses at this college?
   a. Yes   b. No

Index

For more information on civic responsibility and service learning in community colleges, please contact:

American Association of Community Colleges
One Dupont Circle, NW, Suite 410
Washington, DC 20036-1176
Phone: 202/728-0200 ext. 254
Fax: 202/728-2965
E-mail: *grobinson@aacc.nche.edu*
Web: *www.aacc.nche.edu/servicelearning*

To purchase additional copies of this guide, please contact:

Community College Press
P.O. Box 311
Annapolis Junction, MD 20701-0311
Phone: 800/250-6557
Fax: 301/604-0158
E-mail: *aaccpub@pmds.com*
Web: *www.aacc.nche.edu/bookstore*

*A Practical Guide for Integrating
Civic Responsibility into the Curriculum*

Order #1607